THE ART OF THEOLOGICAL REFLECTION

An Ecumenical Study

Ronald Gariboldi
Daniel Novotny

Jean S. Novotny, Editor

UNIVERSITY
PRESS OF
AMERICA

Lanham • New York • London

Copyright © 1987 by

University Press of America,® Inc.

4720 Boston Way
Lanham, MD 20706

3 Henrietta Street
London WC2E 8LU England

British Cataloging in Publication Information Available

Library of Congress Cataloging-in-Publication Data

Gariboldi, Ronald J., 1935-
  The art of theological reflection.

  Bibliography: p.
  1. Theology—Methodology. I. Novotny, Daniel.
II. Novotny, Jean S.   III. Title.
BR118.G29 1987   230'.01'8   87-10385
ISBN 0-8191-6317-1 (alk. paper)
ISBN 0-8191-6318-X (pbk. : alk. paper)

Persons who encourage are embodiments of faith; like Barnabas, the New Testament "son of encouragement," they are realities who set a kind of corporate disposition. Surely, those around us at the time of writing have endured the inthrusting of theologically reflective conversation at every possible moment in committee meeting or class preparation. Particularly, we thank George Sinclair, Chair of the Department of Church and Ministry at Andover Newton, who most persistently encouraged us to put into writing our classroom experiences and whose vision of field education has been taken worldwide by students who have come to study with him and Maria Harris (then Howard Professor of Religious Education at Andover Newton) without whose forthright critique and patient suggestions we would not have continued and whose self-description as "ineluctably and quintessentially our **Roman Catholic** colleague" in a Protestant place has given heart to our journey toward ecumenical sensitivity.

For improvement of style, especially moving from indirect discourse and Latinisms to an active mood, we are indebted to Michael McGarry, currently Rector at St. Paul's College in Washington, D.C. James and Evelyn Whitehead, members of the Associate Faculty at Loyola University with whom Ron has studied, gave time both to read and then write for us; their gracious response kept us at our work.

Some of the writing took place under the hospitality of the Monks of St. Anselm's Abbey in Manchester, New Hampshire; it was the right place for such work.

....
Finally, our pieces of insight were reworked, interleaved, and set up for printing by Jean Novotny; we are glad for her clarity of style and word processing skill.

How do we make sense of our life with God? Sure and steady answers to this question used to be provided for us: no-nonsense catechisms and unambiguous doctrinal statements told us who we were and how we belonged to God. The challenging season of renewal initiated in the Second Vatican Council brought these formulations under review. Old answers seemed no longer to persuade; the center did not hold.

But in this experience of crisis, the Spirit has awakened gifts within the community of faith. We came to realize, again, that we are meant to be co-authors of the religious significance of our lives. As adult believers, we are invited -- even required -- to become active partners in discovering and defending the often illusive meaning of God's love acting in our lives and in our time.

Theological reflection is the ongoing effort to make sense of our life with God. The year 1972 proved to be a watershed, as one approach to theology reached its zenith and another style of reflection was beginning to stir. That year Bernard Lonergan, one of the theological giants of this century, published his magisterial METHOD IN THEOLOGY. Lonergan's method of theological reflection is a gifted example of what we might call the "heroic style" of doing theology. His approach was both highly intellectual and strikingly individual. And these qualities could aptly be used to characterize what mainstream theology -- Catholic and Protestant -- had become: the effort of carefully trained individuals, guided preeminently by the resources of reason and analysis, to grasp and explain Christian faith.

Ensconced in the twin towers of the university and the priesthood, theology was the work of specialists. Their very learning separated them from the religious experience of the "ordinary faithful." These men (and it is important to acknowledge that until the last decade virtually all recognized theologians were men) sought to understand and explain Scripture, Christian history, and the contemporary challenges of faith. The faithful were, at best, beneficiaries of the theological dialogue -- not participants.

In the 1970's, however, another way of doing theology was hesitantly being attempted. Its approach marked a shift from theology as predominantly rational and solitary toward methods more imaginative and shared. Theologians themselves were becoming more intrigued by the role of extra-rational factors -- passion and imagination -- in the experience of faith. What if the emotional arousals of delight and compassion and anger are more than distractions in the process of "faith seeking understanding"? What if their effect is not always to distort, but sometimes to reveal, the action of God? Perhaps the preference for a dispassionate theology is more stoic than Christian.

And as the influence of passion was being re-examined, so was the role of the imagination. Faith itself, theologians were coming to appreciate, is an exercise of the imagination. Christians recognize a pattern and purpose in life that the non-believer "cannot imagine." It is the religious imagination that generates and sustains the extraordinary Christian vision we know as the kingdom of God.

There was new interest as well in the role of the community of faith in the theological task. Historical studies affirmed that groups of believers not only receive the faith; they hand it on in ways that are at once faithful and creative. This realization suggests that theology belongs, properly, within these communities. Perhaps the faithful presentation of the ancient Christian truths -- grace and sin, redemption and forgiveness, loss and new life -- needs a wider range of actors and a more lively contemporary script. This realization makes theology more than a profession; it becomes one of the performing arts. As THE ART OF THEOLOGICAL REFLECTION describes in the chapters ahead, the locale of theology shifts from the tidy but isolated laboratory to the messy and more crowded studio.

Within the American Catholic experience over the past decade, a number of attempts have been made to develop tools and strategies in support of this new trend in theological reflection. In the mid-1970's we ourselves gathered a group of Catholic ministers and theological educators to explore a method of community-based pastoral reflection; the fruit of this discussion appeared in METHOD IN MINISTRY (1979). In 1980 Thomas Groome of Boston College published his influential CHRISTIAN RELIGIOUS EDUCATION, developing an approach to theological reflection rooted in a community's life. Two

Jesuit-related efforts continued this exploration. In TRACING THE SPIRIT (1983) colleagues at the Woodstock Center studied small faith communities and their actual styles of decision-making. That same year Peter Henriot and Joseph Holland published SOCIAL JUSTICE: LINKING FAITH AND JUSTICE, making available the method of reflection they had developed and used so effectively through the Center of Concern.

In THE ART OF THEOLOGICAL REFLECTION Ronald Gariboldi and Daniel Novotny bring the fruits of their own collaboration to this effort to return theology to the community of faith. In touch with the recent developments in Catholic circles, their intent is to serve a wider ecumenical audience. The approach Gariboldi and Novotny take is at once nuanced and practical; it honors imagination as a religious resource and encourages communal reflection as an essential element in Christian decision-making. Their book is a welcome gift to the Church.

James D. Whitehead
Evelyn Eaton Whitehead

THE ART of THEOLOGICAL REFLECTION: An Ecumenical Study

The art of theological reflection begins with the idea that artistry involves the creative participation of a person in the organic nuance of faith. In this book we offer a methodology and a number of resources in addition to our own experiences.

Reflection suggests a stream of thought; within the metaphor of stream, we may travel in different modes. Some of us may travel in a canoe or kayak, others in a rowboat; some require horsepower, others prefer sail. Choice and preference are part of the response of the Christian to the faith and, in the response, they may offer new images for others.

To shift the figure, theological reflection may be seen as a nourishing meal. We try to define the dimensions of that meal. Within those dimensions, there are choices for appetizers, main courses, and desserts. We offer, as well in our book, examples of the portions of the meal which have been nourishing to others. We hope that the variety offered will increase the appetite.

INTRODUCTION

In the foreward of his book, THEOLOGY IN A NEW KEY,[1] Robert McAfee Brown says that the themes which he treats have been forced upon him. He is speaking about the impulsion to take seriously liberation theology as it has reached the United States from Latin America. This theology confronts us with the current struggle of third world Christians and calls for us to reform our lives so that we may learn to see our day-to-day relationships from the side of the poor.

It is with a similar compelling spirit that we undertake this study. Theological reflection could transform the way we teach theology. Enabling Christians, as it often does, to discover both the meaning of the Paschal Mystery and their obligation to work towards the establishment of the Kingdom, theological reflection can result in painful/confrontive or healing/freeing insights.

Theological reflection is a process. Sometimes built on the action-reflection model, it moves from incident to consideration and evaluation; at other times, study and illumination under the prompting of the Holy Spirit lead to activity in mission. Clouded in ambiguity, the term "theological reflection" has sent professors and students in divinity schools, pastors, religious communities, and church leaders on a search for a formula which will seed the cloud of mystery.

Distinctions blur between theology and theological reflection because the reflector begins by considering what has been already given in theology. Through reflection, tenets of theology are not only learned and noted historically; they acquire substance through theoretical application and devotional life, through ethical consideration and cultural confrontation. Indeed, in this way, the body of theology, itself, may be challenged or sustained.

Another blurring occurs in the space between theological reflection and spiritual formation. The discipline of contemplation provides the mood for theological reflection -- a mode of learning -- but in spiritual formation contemplation is a mode of communion -- an act of devotion.

Theological reflection, taking a bridge position between the two "firm" disciplines of theology and spiritual formation, provides a strong, not weak, span. It takes an intermediate stance much like the historian's position between the event and contemporary life. A. M. Fairbairn gives us these following words which apply as much to theological reflection as to history:

> History does not lose but gain in accuracy and truth by being mediately rather than immediately written. The last and most trustworthy historian is not the eyewitness, but the man who can question him and who can through the issue read character, action, and event with greater intelligence than he. The most accurate and informing history is not the diary but the discourse of the writer who sees not simply the salient feature of each person or occurrence, but sees also each thing as it is and all the things together. And when we come to study the Gospels together, we see how much time has done for the perspective which gives to each figure in the scene its due place and proportion.[2]

(Read especially the first lines, replacing the word "history" with the words "theological reflection." Thus "theological reflection does not lose but gain in accuracy and truth by being mediately rather than immediately written. The last and most trustworthy theologian is not the eyewitness, but the (one) who can question ..... and who can through the issue read character, action, and event .....")

Theologians have long been aware that official church documents sanction practices which have arisen from the grassroots.[3] This process is grounded in what has technically become known as the **sensus fidelium**, a source which has frequently led to dogma. Since the time of the Apostolic Church, the Christian community has been attempting to understand the message of Jesus and his apostles and to initiate in a given era the pastoral practices which appropriately embody the Gospel. Hence, as co-authors of this ecumenical study, we do not propose to introduce the reader to a new process but to enable the reader to rediscover a process which is as old as the church. Indeed, theological reflection shares its method with the Gospel writers, themselves.

Through theological reflection the body of Sacred Scripture was developed. In the midst of the turmoil and confusion surrounding the infant church, the followers of Jesus in community began to develop and articulate Jesus' teachings in a way which helped them to live as Christians. These reflections were the sources of Christian tradition as found in the Bible and in the writings of church fathers and mothers.

Karl Rahner has defined the church as "the historical and social presence of God's self-communication to the world in Christ."[4] Each contemporary Christian has to encounter this communication and work out how God's ongoing self-revelation lives in her or him. Our goal, then, is to assist the reader in understanding this process. We will identify the components, expose the theological underpinnings, explore various models, and suggest some practical implications for pastoral ministry.

Out of our experience, specifically in team teaching, we were led to write this book. One of us is a Protestant pastor whose own family were persecuted for holding tenets opposed to Roman Catholicism; the other is a Roman Catholic priest. It seems appropriate that we two should be collaborating in this ecumenical endeavor. We have discovered both what unites us and what divides us. You may notice where we have made the effort of blending and where the effort to blend brought us to an acknowledgment of our inability to agree. Though we hear each other, we move right by each other in the discussion of some issues. In these cases, we have presented parallel essays.

Finally, it is our desire that pastors, students, and all who struggle to discover the meaning of their Christian call will find in this work a source of challenge and a tool to assist them in their own process of reflection.

Ronald Gariboldi,
St. John's Seminary

Daniel Novotny,
Andover Newton Theological School

First Part: THE STUDIO in WHICH WE WORK

Theological reflection is an art more at home in
the studio than the laboratory. It takes its shape from
1.) the matter, itself, that is brought for reflection,
2.) the occasions which provide the opportunity to enter
into the process, 3.) the theological context within
which the process is situated, and 4.) the terminology
for discourse.

Section One will consider the meaning of
language, the matter for reflection, some appropriate
occasions for engaging in the process, and the
theological milieu.

1

Chapter 1
Process and Language

A DEFINITION OF THEOLOGICAL REFLECTION

We define theological reflection first by distinguishing it from what it is not. It is not systematic or historical theology. Schubert M. Ogden, in a classic article entitled "What is Theology?" defines Christian theology as "the fully reflected understanding of the Christian witness of faith as decisive for human existence." [1] Inside this definition, systematic theology expresses the reality of faith itself; historical theology describes this faith's development within a particular historical context. [2] Thus, theology addresses ultimate questions and systematic theology presents that work with a coherent system or argument. Historical theology takes the perspective of the past, of the tradition, of the experience in church and church councils and presents it chronologically. Both systematic and historical Christian theology depend upon the Hebrew Bible and the New Testament, particularly the life and teachings of Jesus Christ.

Pastoral theology viewed within this context serves theology by reflecting upon these ultimate questions in a present situation. It has as its goal pastoral action that is informed by systematic and historical theology. Theological reflection as a mode of pastoral theology, then, engages the church as a community of believers in a disciplined reflection upon ultimate questions. The reality of faith expressed in systematic theology, the development of this faith expressed in historical theology, and the concerns of this faith expressed in pastoral theology are all brought to the present experience of the church.

Additionally, theological reflection is a method. It wants to see theology reflected in the living water of worship. It takes as seriously the dimension of poetry as of prose, of aesthetics as of systematics. Thus, the way of knowing represented by an organ fugue, a cathedral by Christopher Wren, the prayers of the desert fathers, and the silence of the Trappist devotion may be as significant for theological reflection as the arguments of Aquinas or Calvin. Theological reflection is the conscious effort to bring together all human re-

3

sources in the study about God.

THE LANGUAGE

No matter how we speak about God, the descriptive language we use cannot escape change. Even in any given moment, God's nature always eludes description, taut and precious as our language may be. Inherent in language is its limited capacity for describing the world as it is seen; how much more limited it is in describing infinite reality. We recognize humanity's inability to give true expression; yet that effort cannot be abandoned.

Language is peculiar to humans. Words exercise power, especially the powers of composing and relating, of creation and compassion. Although animals, birds, and dolphins communicate, words are peculiar gifts to humankind. Words nurture the mind and spirit just as bread nourishes the body.

Religious writing starts, as Frost said poems do, with a lump in the throat, a deep ache in the psyche.[3] Often the best writing knows what it cannot say and ends with a seeming contradiction which, in fact, reveals truth. It is paradoxical.

A paradox challenges sluggish thought processes by offering the surprise that stimulates fresh insights. Jesus, in his short, pungent, and often cryptic answers to his inquirers, offered to receptive minds seeds that later matured to faith. In paradoxical epigrams, he challenged Thomas and Nicodemus, Mary and Martha to respond with caring and commitment. In our language we are often tempted to make reality more articulate than it is -- fuller, wordier, longer. It is indeed obvious that without some form of language, existence would be hidden and mute. But only when words come up fresh and breathless, come up still moist and glistening from the sea of existence, do they carry power and authority.

A physicist would say that every word spoken sets in motion a minute change having endless ramifications in the physical universe. The theologian would say the same thing about the breaking of bread in the Lord's Supper; it, too, is an act with physical ramifications, but theologically it is an immeasurable act with timeless repercussions. When one person speaks to another, their corporate act affects not only the two of them but in ever wider reverberation affects others' lives as well.

Religious words start with awe. Moses in Midian, Paul on that dusty road, Jesus in the Jordan -- each of them reports something that is poorly represented by words such as "the voice of God" or "the moving of the Spirit." "Shalom," "oneness," even "God," are pallid metaphors of the experience. It is only long after this effort to name that religion expands to include the many words of ethics, dogma, institution, and ritual.

Gospel life is not merely intellectual exercise but experience in a community of love and forgiveness. Found through theological reflection, insights about the Gospel, both joyful and heartrending, lead to its most stark and realistic utterances, giving character and substance to the events of life. In some denominations the experience of Christian life is visible through a sacramental system and a particular form of ecclesial life. In others, it is left to the leader of worship or the believer, alone, to find the words for adoration, praise, and communion.

Christians believe that through faith and baptism they are born into a community of love and forgiveness that has been disclosed in the primordial vision of creativity and in the ultimate vision of God's perfection. Theological reflection recalls that we are born into a world of insensitivity, tears and cruelty, of narrow loyalties and strife, of bitterness, self-striving, pride and competition. But it knows equally a world full of sisterly and brotherly love, forgiveness, joy, and compassion. In short, we are born into a situation of sickness and health, of decay and growth, of despair and hope. Such thinking leads people to understand and restate for our time the meaning of doctrinal statements.

Living and dying and the human responses to them are complex. It is alluring to believe that intellectual inquiry somehow makes them less complex. Of course, this is not so. Living and dying happen; they are life itself. Theological reflection cannot remain in the intellect alone; it must touch also the heart and will. Loved by God, the human person is given the freedom to decide how to live and how to die. Ultimate decisions, influenced by individual experience, find their substance in an ability to say "yes" or "no" to the divine offer of love.

Far more important than any phrase or formulation, however rich in association, is the capacity to wait in a state of attention, cultivating the faculties of love, hope, and faith, resisting as best one can that desire for certainty which seems to be one of humankind's strongest impulses and a principal cause of its most constant errors.

JESUS, THE "WORD OF GOD"

The contents of Jesus' teaching come to us in an indirect and often ambiguous manner. Their historical and textual ambiguity stresses their "innate" authority, just as the general uncertainty as to their context warns us against giving them too local a habitation and a name. Though specific because told through incident (story), the teachings retain texture and depth. As every fibre of worsted fabric, in contrast to satin fabric, cannot be felt at a single touch, Jesus' teachings cannot be grasped as though they are single-dimensioned. It is the nature of worsted fabric, as of paradoxical teaching, to be thick and over-layered.

The words of Jesus do not point to a "truth." They are Truth. Furthermore, we can say that Jesus IS the sum of his words, that he is "the Word" and that today he lives in his words.

It is our dilemma that we do not know how to live. At our best, we have the courage to experiment, explore, risk. The words of Jesus support us in our quest, helping us to understand our human condition as the beginning of comprehension. When we seek, Jesus' words promise that we shall find. When we ask, we shall be answered, and when we knock, the door will be opened to us.

Just as the ultimate justification of the Iliad does not lie in its Homeric parentage but in its beauty, so the question of the authenticity of Jesus' words is ultimately not the scholar's problem. It is not a question of authorship but of truth and beauty. The "words" expressed in theological reflection should lead to "the Word." They must be rooted in Truth and find their service in the continuous incarnation of God through the actions of humankind.

The two-edged sword of the Word -- which both judges and redeems us -- is more than our words. This caution of judgment stands before Christians who enter

6

into theological reflection. It calls for courage in examining our convictions by the light of tradition, scripture, others' faith, and the contemporary situation. The Christian is tired of hearing about public leaders with the "courage of their convictions." Nero, Caligula, Attila, and Hitler had the courage of their convictions; they did not have the courage to examine their convictions or to change them. Sincerity may mean no more than that one has persuaded oneself. Conviction needs a referent outside of self. Theological reflection may provide this reference point.

We discover the fruit of theological reflection in the pastoral response of individuals and communities who enflesh the Gospel by acting compassionately, by surrendering self for the sake of the "Word," and by challenging the world to work for the establishment of the Kingdom of God.

Theology is the study of God through the theological endeavors of systematic, biblical-historical, and pastoral theology. The process of theological reflection is at the service of these theological endeavors.

THEOLOGY AND THEOLOGICAL REFLECTION

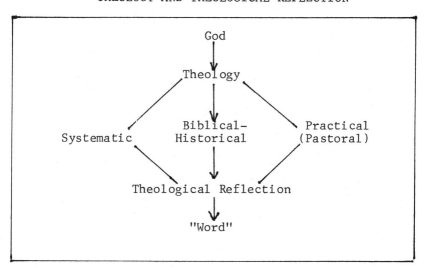

Figure 1

Chapter 2
Matter for Theological Reflection

CHRISTIAN IDENTITY and the CHURCH

Again and again, we will be saying that theological reflection is a process; it is an art. Its matter is dependent upon its goal. Primarily, that goal is to assist the Christian to discover, through theory and practice, the meaning of the Christian life. We want to underline that it is through the process that understanding comes.

For theological reflection the goal is, in actuality, twofold. The first is the formation of the Christian, and the second is the Christian's relationship to humanity. It is only when Christians discover their identity in Jesus Christ that they can enter fully into the redemptive mission of the Church. Healing, sustaining, guiding, communicating, and organizing are the traditional modes of organizing the Church's pastoral presence.[1]

Motivated by the Church as harbinger of the Kingdom, theological reflection sits in the center of mission. It begins with the meaning of membership in the Church and the essential linkage to mission. The Church is not the Kingdom; it is the first sign of the Kingdom. In pointing the way, one ecclesiastical tradition focuses upon community and another functions primarily as a sacrament; both intend to look ahead to the Kingdom and at the same time render it present (the tension between the already and the not-yet).

THE MATTER of EXPERIENCE

The matrix of experience -- relationships, intellectual activity, the body of faith, and the spiritual life -- is the "stuff" of reflection. Christians reflect theologically upon human existence, especially those moments of "ultimate concern."[2] Thus, in the lives of Christians, incidents occur which either enhance commitment or raise doubts. It is through these times of faith's seeking understanding that theology becomes both personal and, when shared, ecclesial. Faith is equally individual and societal.

9

THE MATTER of RELATIONSHIPS between INDIVIDUALS

In the Christian sense, relationships between individuals are not simply ordinary commerce, one to the other, but are relationships built on concern for the other. Joseph Conrad wrote that "for life to be full and large it must contain the care of the past and of the future in every passing moment of the present."[3] Caring is the dimension of ethics towards which theology points when it remembers that God has created humanity in God's own image and likeness.

Milton Mayeroff in his work, ON CARING,[4] has said, "To care for another person in the most significant sense is to help him grow and actualize himself.... ..... to help another person grow is at least to help him care for something or someone apart from himself, and it involves encouraging and assisting him to find and create areas of his own in which he is able to care."

This definition stands in contrast to the notion that caring is the complete giving of oneself to another. Such surrender has the effect of smothering the other and creating a barrier to growth. No. The caring person becomes the facilitator for the other to break through the encapsulating shell of self-love and to find escape from narcissism. Moreover, in its mutuality, a caring relationship allows the facilitator, too, to actualize self.[5] True caring involves some form of reciprocity.

In the dynamics of caring, one problem is to locate the balance between self-seeking and self-sacrifice.[6] Tension pulls at these poles. It is evident from Mayeroff's work that in being needed, one experiences a feeling of belonging and often of peace.[7]

A caring relationship can be a dynamic process in which two people find a measure of self-actualization and both experience need for another's love. By calling this kind of caring a "dynamic force," we focus upon movement toward self-fulfillment, but we are not here speaking of fulfillment in isolation. Christians find true fulfillment only in receiving another's offer of love. The mutuality cannot be overstressed. If this return of love is fostered and not blocked by an eagerness to be all-giving and unreceptive, the resulting relationship of caring can unlock the prison of self-love.

To carry that metaphor into a case study, we

offer the following illustration of an actual prison situation. It presents the struggle of a Roman Catholic priest with a pastoral relationship in prison ministry.

Letters from Prison

For a two-month period, I relieved the regular chaplain who had gone on study leave. In this interim commitment of weekly visits, I interviewed new inmates and visited the hospital and protective custody units.

Except for the intake sessions, the ministry was largely sacramental; it developed that the major source of our pastoral contact was the celebration of Mass. The following excerpts are from letters I received from one inmate. He is 26 years old, married with two children. After a period of his imprisonment, his wife left him and he attempted suicide.

Sept. 4: "Hope these few lines find you in the best of health and want to say we all miss you very much. And hope you will come back and see us again. I'm doing OK here; things are still the same (Oh, well). Father, why I'm writing you is asking if you maybe could get people out there to write me; it's very lonely lying here and getting mail really helps."

Sept. 22: "Thanks for writing to me ..... I will pray for you every night ..... you can count on that. As for me, I'm doing all right, I guess (could be better) ..... Things here are still the same and we do the same things day in and day out. I hope you can make it out here again because we all miss you very much. (I do.)"

When I received these two letters, I was surprised at his apparent fondness of me because I as celebrant of the Eucharist had been able to have little personal contact with him. What did he see in me? I decided that I would try to visit him but I found it difficult to find time. Though I wrote and told him I would try to visit him, when the day came I found

11

it was impossible.

Oct. 8: "Did something come up last Thursday that you didn't make it up here? Sorry that it is taking me so long to write you back, but there's been a lot of things going wrong for me right now. D. got into a fight the other day with another guy. He's all right, though ..... Well, it's getting late so I'm going to close for now; so you take care and God bless you!!! P.S. I'm always praying for you!!!"

Oct. 18: "Just a few lines to say thanks for taking time out to come and see me! I feel so good when I can talk with you. Will be looking forward to seeing you soon (I hope.)"

All his letters finish with "God bless you!!! I'm always praying for you. Love Ya!!!" He has also sent me a card saying "Jesus in Me Loves You!" Another card said "Within each heart there is some portion of loneliness......that stretches across life's seasons......as a spider web stretches across the grasses..."

REFLECTION: I am caught! Can my visits to the prison be my prayer and my contact with Jesus? Can I offer them as my contemplation? What about my personal struggle with a workaholic syndrome? Is the truth in that card, "Jesus in Me Loves You" the real evidence of the indwelling Holy Spirit?

I wonder if my work can serve as a source of my spirituality. I read something about one of Mother Theresa's sisters who was ecstatic about her experience of meeting Jesus as she washed the worm-infested sores of a dying man.

I shall have to look more closely at my schedule and allow some time for such a ministry. My prayer time does not always have to be in quiet before the Blessed Sacrament.

I am also humbled when I see how Jesus can shine through me in the celebration

12

of the Mass. I am now more aware than I
ever was of the sacredness of what I do
when I celebrate the Eucharist.

Some administrative issues in this case:
- What is the continuing responsibility of a pastor who
has been brought in for an interim period?
- What responsibility, if any, does the interim priest
have NOT to continue visiting because the work is no
longer his?

Pastoral issues in this case:
- Is there, beyond the professional call, a human responsibility to maintain, for his brother, a friendly
link with humanity?
- The particularly priestly function here of carrying
the sacrament to the one in need is awesome. How does
the human being who is priest accept this?
- In what way in this story is the inmate ministering to
the priest?
- Where is the mutuality of caring as Mayeroff has described it?

INDIVIDUALS and STRUCTURES in SOCIETY
Many of us who reflect theologically are engaged
in pastoral planning, any form of which necessitates social analysis as well. The matter for reflection is often both spiritual and political.

A pastoral supervisor recorded the following incident in which were raised for the student significant
questions around an issue of social injustice. The case
illustrates how experience joins intellectual understanding and moral decision. It is rooted in the conscientious struggles with unjust structures. But it also
presents another level of reflection: what is the moral
obligation of obedience to authority within Church
structure?

Obedience
Tom, an intern at St. Rose Parish, had
already confronted social justice concerns. So when he read an issue of **Maryknoll Magazine** which described the exe-
cution of four women in El Salvador, he
wanted to find ways to raise the con-
sciousness of St. Rose's parishioners.
It was his moral obligation, he believed, to increase awareness of the

13

fact that the financial aid of the U.S. Government to El Salvador was indirectly supporting such brutality. He hoped that as Christians the members of the community would contact their representatives and register their concern. He planned to bring this material through the vehicle of a 15 minute film.

The Pastor of the Parish forbade the film's showing, apparently because planning had not sufficiently prepared the members to understand the issues.

The Problem:
Does the intern obey the Pastor who has authority over him? What are some of his internal struggles? What about his moral responsibility to conscience? How does one handle the issue of pastoral integrity and pastoral practice?

The supervisor and student used an article, excerpted below, as a starting point for their session:

"Obedience is, generally speaking, a recognition of legitimate authority which must be expressed in one's opinions and behavior." Three points are made:
(a) "..... obedience in Scripture chiefly means submission to the 'it must be' of saving history
(Mt. 16:21).
(b) "..... there arises the difficult question of how we know that subjecting ourselves to a human authority is the most thoroughgoing obedience to God. (But)..... obedience is an essential part of permanent commitment to a particular form of life in the Church. A formal obedience for obedience's sake is of no moral value; obedience does not give a superior a blank cheque. Rather it is the acceptance of a common religious life under constitutions which the Church has approved as a true and possible expression of a life devoted to God, agreeable to the doctrine and example of Christ, as acceptance of an in-

14

calculable destiny ..... It is, of course, very difficult to distinguish a command which is objectively mistaken from one that is immoral. In view of this difficulty it is downright un-Christian to fall back on the amoral maxim that 'orders are orders;' rather the subject has a duty openly to resist authority if it requires what is plainly absurd .....
(c) What we have said applies equally to the canonical obedience of a person appointed to ecclesiastical office." [8]

During theological reflection, both supervisor and future minister looked at the virtue of obedience, an issue which could have been obscured by the emotional issue of the public witness for demands of justice.

The intern was able to see that blind obedience was not demanded. Here, obedience was suggested because the Pastor knew the complexities of the parish and because precipitous action by the intern could have created more indignation than movement towards justice. The intern was able to recognize that transformation necessitates patient education. Social justice, structural change, and a decision requiring obedience were all part of an experience providing grist for theological reflection.

(Examined by pastor and intern in another tradition, this case might uncover a different set of issues. Maybe it would not look like an obedience issue but a pedagogical one -- how do pastors transmit experience to interns learning from them? Or they might decide that justice is such an overriding concern it ought not be regarded within any other context but justice, itself -- that in this case authority was secondary to justice. They could together decide that strategy and the wisdom of group experience dictate caution, yes, but they would urge that, indeed in this instance, the action of showing the film should be taken.)

Obedience has ethical boundaries. The world does not understand the mystical sweetness of obeying human authority which has been given sanction by the Church as God's authority. Luther, even when he broke with authority, was able to say that obedience, while it is a means to orderliness, is also an obligation to God. To think

15

of self as under authority unifies worth, signifies createdness, provides stature.

Under the spotlight of recent world history especially, religious strands separate over the kind of authority which builds up or diminishes, over the uses to which authority is put, and over the determination with which obedience is invested. Configurations such as partnership or collegiality depend on mutual consent and are introduced to move away from the label of authority. Clothed in softer terms like "responsibility" or "leadership," authority can nevertheless be domineering, so it is a religious issue that they be transformed into life-enhancing and not life-threatening terms. Looking for the innuendo in these issues is the matter for theological reflection.

Obedience to the will of God must take seriously our propensity for identifying our will with God's will. Clearly, the Gospel always proclaims by word and deed but never outside the common life of a group. All group life requires loyalty and a degree of authority and obedience. But group life -- especially, we think, Christian group life -- requires a margin of change, of yearning for the transcendent which can never be fully grasped. There is something rigid about it and yet something very supple. Christian faith does not smoothe out the difficulties of thinking and acting, but it makes them bearable and offers means whereby human beings can provide enough order and law over the chaos of thinking and feeling to make possible significant living. The Christian faith is authoritative for the Christian, proclaiming the virtue of self denial for a larger good.

Obedience in this sense is between loved ones, between friends. When affection is strong, friends give one another authority and they obey one another. This authority and this obedience mirror the relationship of God and humanity when God delegates authority to humans as a friend would to friends.

THE MATTER of STUDY
In attempts to identify experiences which can serve as valid sources for theological reflection, academic research is often forgotten or labeled "merely academic," not expected to eventuate in doing. Yet pungent writing has just as often led a reader to active engagement.

16

A pastor writes in his journal:
"In my theological journey, I found that the writings of a major Roman Catholic theologian, Karl Rahner, greatly influenced me in my style of ministry. An article by Rahner entitled 'Reflection on the Unity of the Love of Neighbor and the Love of God'[9] became a turning point in my practice of ministry. It led me to research his theological system. Because of this research, I was able to look at my ministry in terms which dealt with mystery and the presence of the transcendent. I was able to articulate my ministerial goals in a way which not only appealed to my affective capacities but also to my intellectual capacities. This theoretical text became a source for naming and understanding my experience."

In similar fashion, a Protestant minister took a reflective reading of Langdon Gilkey's HOW THE CHURCH CAN MINISTER TO THE WORLD WITHOUT LOSING ITSELF[10] -- wherein Protestantism is challenged to rediscover the place of the transcendent -- and reoriented, with them, the life and worship of the congregation.

SUBJECT MATTER in the BODY of FAITH
The Body of Faith -- that is, written statements and acts of worship -- as matters for theological reflection can be entirely theoretical, but when this is the case there is sterility. The case method and accompanying plan of mission, then, provide zest.

The prison chaplain already described, a Roman Catholic, illustrates a pastoral approach within the tradition of Sacramental Ministry. He concentrated on a personal description of his ministry and in being so concerned with himself, he failed to recognize important instruments of redemption. While it is true that the Gospel is carried in human vessels and frequently is thus diminished or marred, persons are not the only vessels. God is not lost when we fail. Liturgy reveals God's loving care; at times a homily explicates beyond the human capacity of the speaker; priestliness (in both conformist and non-conformist traditions) is the awesome quality of ordination; the Church, herself -- in the stunning quality of her architecture and adornment -- points beyond our "poor power to add or detract."

The intern's experience as he responds to social

17

injustice, meets the challenge of authority within hier-
archical churches. Individual authority faces structural
authority. These situations require knowledge of scripture and church policy and a pastoral response rooted in
the Gospel.

Taken purely theoretically, the Body of Faith
can become a gameboard on which theological reflectors
play out their interests. But true reflection begins
with devotional ministry and ends in decision. Insights
stimulate intellect; human plight moves the heart; intellectual and spiritual stimulation substantially enhance élan.

Dorothee Soelle provides a caution that exactly
underscores a diabolical quality that arises when we
stop at reflection-only without continuing to appropriate mission She says:

> ..... the danger of the middle-class
> situation is eternal indecision. Kierke-
> gaard criticized this type of person un-
> der the heading of 'endless reflection,'
> which makes a person incapable of arriv-
> ing at a decision and facing up to real-
> ity. The intellectual and religious neu-
> trality which fears to make a decision
> for or against faith and continually
> puts the decision off is not very far
> removed from the intellectual and poli-
> tical neutrality by means of which an
> intellectual tries to keep out of con-
> flicts .....[11]

THE MATTER of SPIRITUAL LIFE
Distinctions between counseling and spiritual
direction draw continual debate. The important aspect
is, however, that these two means of guidance can support each other. The following definitions of human personality, drawn from psychology and theology, indicate
complementarity:

Viktor E. Frankl[12] conceives of the human personality as "based on three pillars -- the freedom of will,
the will to meaning, and the meaning of life."

Karl Rahner and Herbert Vergrimler define personality in THE THEOLOGICAL DICTIONARY[13] in the following
words:

In an ethical sense, personality may be said to be present when a human being's free decision really and unflinchingly accepts the fact that he is a person, accepts the dialogical character of life ordered to mystery, accepts freedom, duty, responsibility, unrepressed sinfulness, his neighbor's ineffable individuality, pain, and death. Complete personality is rooted in the genius of the heart, not of the intellect.

Thus, at least these psychological and theological definitions of personality are compatible. Both accept, as components of the human personality, freedom, the will to find meaning in the exigencies of life, and the search for the ultimate purpose for existence.

If it is accepted that the focus of theological reflection is on Christian formation in relationship to the Church's mission, then the psychological and the spiritual levels of personality are its matter as well. Our previously cited examples of the prison chaplain and the intern could also have been examined under this rubric.

THE MATTER of FREEDOM
The prison chaplain struggled with psychological freedom because he felt caught by priestly demands. Beyond the external forces limiting his freedom, he was shackled by a false concept of spirituality that inhibited his ability to experience the presence of God in action as well as in contemplative prayer. Christians discover the face of God everywhere -- in the human situation, in activity, and in quiet. It is freeing to conclude that communion with God is not restricted to moments of prayer.

Some structures are barriers to human freedom; others are not. The intern believed he was trapped by a structure that felt like stricture. His was the dilemma of discernment between authority that frees for proper action and authority that protects for institutional longevity.

Throughout the cases cited, there is an urge towards meaning. No one in ministry wants to look back on the work of the day and see no accomplishment in it. The very effort of ministry implies a will to do something

19

that communicates good, that releases meaning for giver
and receiver.

In his narration the prison chaplain indicates
that he was deeply moved by the account of a religious
woman who was ecstatic when she washed the worm-infested
sores of a dying man. Should he -- can he -- feel that
way about his own ministry? He is searching for meaning
in his ministry to the imprisoned. He hears his own culture tell him that such a ministry is marginal. He hears
his Church's theology say that meaning is in the celebration of liturgy and the experience of others. Does
that include experiences like hers -- Mother Theresa's
helper? Is he prepared to meet God in that way?

In the intern's attempt to understand obedience
as virtue, there is no gain if the authority, itself, is
unjust. Submission of one's will to another is often
emotionally disturbing and a block to meaning. Yet, when
we submit our own will to the needs of another, there is
meaning in obedience. It, obedience, no longer flows
from the weak towards the powerful; it flows from both
persons to the situation of need. It comes closer to
partnership. Theological reflection looks for these
ways.

THE MATTER of SPIRITUAL FORMATION
Spiritual life is sacred, and reflection times
are holy -- but not more holy than the rest of our God-
given life. It is a fact that as we bring all of ourselves into theological reflection, we are bringing our
psychological and spiritual selves, our developed and
embryonic selves, our overt and hidden selves.

Reflection upon only experience and faithfulness
without considering the personality at psychic and spiritual levels would not enable Christian growth or response to mission. So theological reflection regards
spiritual formation but it does not end, as would work
with a spiritual director, with a quest for firmer di-
vine-human encounter.

20

THEOLOGICAL REFLECTION as a DYNAMIC PROCESS

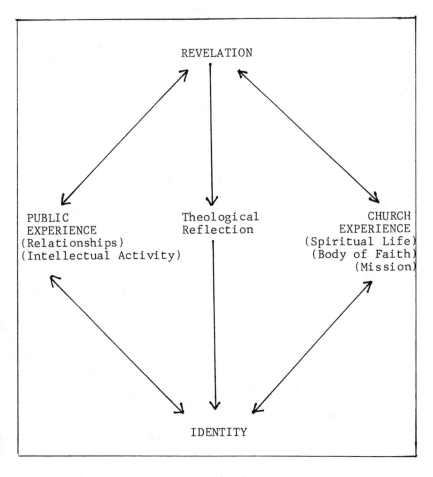

REVELATION

PUBLIC
EXPERIENCE
(Relationships)
(Intellectual Activity)

Theological
Reflection

CHURCH
EXPERIENCE
(Spiritual Life)
(Body of Faith)
(Mission)

IDENTITY

Figure 2

21

Chapter 3
Occasions for Theological Reflection

If theological reflection is about all of experience, then occasions for reflection are not limited to those we consider "theological." As the movements of the Spirit are mysterious, so are the occasions for theological reflection surprising. Requirements are few: 1.)openness to God's presence, 2.)desire to enhance personal response in faith and 3.)intention to assist mission.

We want to go beyond the revered and traditional moments of private contemplation or prayer groups. All pastoral encounters, all moments of sadness and pleasure, all spaces filled with question or assurance are on the threshold of reflection. Ministry increases when the door is opened and thoughtful probing steps into the occasions. Thus, theological reflection is not contemplative prayer; it is not pastoral ministry; it is not worship. It undulates through them; it precedes and follows them.

The following occasions are indicators of the ways in which Christian life provides space for theological reflection. Some are well-known; in others, you may see through your own creativity the ubiquitous quality of reflection.

THE OCCASION OF WORSHIP

Overpowering moments of gratitude, wonder, sorrow, and doubt can be worship times -- private moments or ones ritualized within community. The gift of life itself calls forth gratitude, the realization that without the sustaining power and love of God there would be no human existence.

After a serious operation a woman said to the Roman Catholic hospital chaplain, "When you came to visit me before my operation, it was as though God had come." Such depth of feeling could itself be worship, the expression of her profound thanks. Each had a private reflection -- she, of God's providential care and the chaplain, of the

23

reality of his call.

Groups as well as individuals come to common realizations that are powerful goads for reflection.

During the course of a regional charismatic conference two thousand people listened to a twelve-year-old Mexican girl's story of the feeling of poverty, and they heard American Indians discuss life on a Maine reservation where they are victims of implicit prejudice. In the realization that each person contributes to the world's evil, those worshippers asked forgiveness. Two thousand persons prayed not only for the victims but for themselves, the sources of oppression and prejudice.

Acts of thanksgiving often erupt in the sight of life's natural grandeur, giving way to thoughts of the Creator's power and might. For example, the only suitable response to the sight of Mount Saint Helens, standing in decapitated splendor, or of Oregon's snowcapped Mount Hood, is the flow of awed envelopment which is at once both worship and reflection.

The spontaneous call to God from the petitioner in trouble is frequently a little act of worship preceding the search for meaning.

A man dying of cancer prays for healing and when that does not happen, he prays that through his illness and death he may witness to his family. This prayer has transformed his illness into an occasion for faith's renewal, not alone for him, but for those around him.

Prayers of petition acknowledge the Creator's power and express the believer's humility and trust.

In worship, experience is brought into prayer. Pastors accept this responsibility when they lead a congregation through adoration, contrition, thanksgiving, and supplication. If these words touch the worshipper, they do so because the pastor has pondered those lives, the circumstances of that very congregation.

For example, one pastor enters his church at dusk some evenings to sit in the pews where his people sit and try to understand, no, to feel life from their perspective. What does it feel like to be alone and old?

24

What must a person go through when the verdict of a terminal illness is given? For this newly-married couple, what are the visions of life together they bring to the altar? To sense what they sense, to breathe where they breathe, makes of the pastoral prayer or the communion invitation living words, refreshment for souls crying for God.

Worship is not an impersonal gesture. Joys and sorrows, the realities of oppression and prejudice, the fear of nuclear holocaust, the love of family and friends -- all of life is brought before God in worship.

OCCASIONS OF REFLECTIVE READINGS
Readers of theology look for new ideas, support for positions previously held, continuing education, and intellectual fulfillment. Pondering these same works, though, can touch the dimensions of both private devotion and public worship.

Reflective theological reading may be occasional. Insomnia or a snowbound hiatus, coming unbidden, adjust the angle at which reflection penetrates. Yet, luxurious as these moments of surprise away from routine may be, many people find reading most productive when it is regular and disciplined. It does not have to be solitary. Often pastors with members of a congregation, seminarians with their pastoral supervisors, adult education groups, or colleagues in ministry agree to read the same material. Discussing common readings leads to insights about Christian living.

OCCASIONS OF PREPARATION FOR PUBLIC PRESENTATIONS
For those whose church ministry is a vocation, public presentations and concrete acts of ministry are a way of life. The necessity for study in scripture and history, as well as literature, elicits theological reflection. The weekly discipline of developing lectionary readings with the rhythm of the year is a recurring source of enrichment for conscientious ministers. The Holy Seasons -- Advent and Lent, Holy Week and Pentecost -- are paradigms for the rhythm of one's own devotional life.

Special events confront the worship leader with a shift of view; in funeral or memorial services, marriage or baptismal services, the intent is to be personal and the reflection evokes internalized theological meaning. More stately events, often overlooked opportunities, are periods of preparation for ordination and installation papers; both private and shared work for these occasions is meant to be not only a review of studies taken but of growth marked.

Christian educators, through imaginative reflection on both the material and the persons to be taught, become embodied curricula. They, themselves, are frequently the "lesson," as students perceive the material through them. This calls for clarity between espoused views and style because students are quick to note incongruity between doctrine taught and doctrine enacted.

The preparation of volunteers who visit hospitals and nursing homes is a stimulus for a pastoral reflection on suffering and death's meaning. Confronted daily by despair, loneliness, and death, hospital and prison chaplains contend with the promise of home that all these conditions long for. Unless they are numbed to the milieu, these people are working in the midst of essential probing.

OCCASIONS OF CRISIS
Birth and death, baptism and first communion, marriage and confirmation are all, in one sense, crises. Certainly, they score high in stress. The unplanned and the unexpected, the accident, the sharp surge of sudden anger, the quick moment of comedy and laughter -- all these, too, are crisis times.

The original meaning of "crisis," -- decision -- still holds today. Every personal and social crisis requires decision which in turn determines whether and how we are affected by the crisis. Few serious-minded persons go through life without striving for higher possibilities and grappling with questions of ultimate destiny, looking for their relationship to the Supreme. Such experiences are commonly associated with negotiating important transitions and with solving problems of major importance. Indeed, Dr. Anton Boisen said that a principle religious experience arises under the pressure of crisis whereas in the normal states of mind we tend to think sluggishly in an accepted currency of ideas.[1] In time of crisis, processes speed up; one stands face to face with ultimate realities, and religion comes alive. Meaning outstrips the available symbol and we seek new words to express new ideas which come pulsing in.

The following personal reflection illustrates the way in which a crisis allowed this priest to see again God's providential care.

> After my father's hip had been broken and gangrene set in, the doctors offered a prognosis of double amputation. At the same time, my mother was hospitalized with congestive heart failure. I was facing the threat in every direction....
> - loss of parents as I'd known them -- maybe, even, their deaths.
> - long-suffering crises in their adjustments to pain and limited circumstances
> - my own helplessness to change conditions
> - my guilt that the most immanent crisis was over my own work. Could I continue it, and was I right to make it so high a priority?

Indeed, I was not in control because so much decision-making was over medical details. But surely, my faith had taught me about these moments. Did I believe?
And in the crisis, I knew that God's providence did, in the real life situation, mean that we would all be cared for -- somehow. I put myself in God's care.

> Shortly afterward, my father died unexpectedly in cardiac arrest. Mother, released from the hospital, began to grow dependent upon me.

"Of course," I thought, "she is weakened physically, and she has had an incalculable loss." Again, though, I saw this in my terms, as well. Was this the moment when I would be called to set aside vocation for family?

> Within a period of two weeks Mother was able on her own to decide about leaving the nursing home and receiving care at home. She is relatively happy and no longer dependent upon me.

"Ah", I said to myself at the end, "but things have worked out all right for you. You have a wonderfully adaptable mother who has come through this well and has not asked for the sacrifice of your vocation. Is this what you call God's providence?"

And I came to understand that, yes, my parents were instruments of God's care of me -- even now as they had needed me more than I needed them. I knew again that the nurture we had known among the three of us had brought us to this time when each had been called to particular suffering. And I thanked God for my father's bravery and the fact that he had been spared further pain; I thanked God that I could once again witness my mother's strength and courage; and I thanked God that I had been called to the brink of new decision-making about my vocation. All this had strengthened me, and I prayed for fortitude in continuing as my mother's support.

A crisis moment had become a kairos moment -- that moment unbound by time when significant meaning is captured.[2]

Crisis nearly always connotes negative experience. A crisis usually happens to us and it often requires unwelcome choices. Either we do not want to face the event, or we do not want to make the choice that is implied. But if crisis is, as Boisen suggested, the time at which principle religious experience arises, we want to look at it carefully. Can we approach it with possibility, even while it is disheartening, knowing that if we handle it well we may know something profound? Rollo May writes that because form is the state the human being strives to achieve, we want to take experience -- often chaotic -- and shape it, arrange it, grasp it. So in crisis, we want the time to end; we want the challenge to be resolved.

Certainly, there are crises that must end. Pain must be lessened. Fear must be controlled. Anxiety and unrelieved tension must be dissipated. But there is a quality to some chaotic circumstances, to a few crises, that is prelude to insight. "There is a danger in erasing chaos too easily, for it takes away one's stimulation."[3] We only create when we are compelled by the observance of chaos to make some form. If all were in order, there would be little invitation to work the imagination.

28

So in theological reflection, part of the discernment is to separate genuine dead-ends of crisis (when meaning is gone and alleviation must happen) from apparent blocks that may in fact be the ingredients of chaos which we should bring into shape only partially as we allow our experience and imagination to show us the continuing bubbling of chaos which is our vitality.

OCCASIONS OF HUMOR

As Reinhold Niebuhr has pointed out, both tragedy and comedy are responses to the incongruities of life.[4] Tragedy is the more profound response. At such times we can say only, "My God, my God, why?" A pastor can try to bring imagination and compassion together in the deliberate effort not only to understand others but literally to "sit where they sit" and be overwhelmed. Tragedy can be the beginning of reflection that is "arcane and theological." Niebuhr says that this sense of tragedy is the presence of the Almighty in the holy of holies.

The outer vestibule of the holy of holies, he says, can be humor. "Humor is, in fact, a prelude to faith, and laughter is the beginning of prayer." Psalm 2:4 tells us "He that sitteth in the heavens shall laugh; the Lord shall have them in derision."

There is the suggestion of humor in the sayings of Jesus about swallowing a camel, hair and all, or washing a cup on the outside and leaving the inside unclean.

Humor is the essential ingredient of a faith that takes seriously both the transcendence of God and our human nature. When we realize how quaint we are, how droll our ambitions, we become more sane and whole. To laugh at ourselves is the unique human capacity for self-transcendence. When we stand outside ourselves, it is an immense benefit. Our puffed-up pride and touchy self-importance vanish for a bit.

Theological reflection cannot be mature if it does not accept contradiction. Laughter and tears do not seem to go together, but we know that they do go together.

Pastorally, we have seen a newly-bereaved widow interrupt her grief to laugh at the antics of her child. A sadly morose young person sits on

29

a beach and gets silly with her peers, then
reverts to dejection. Some humor at such times
looks hysterical, but we recognize that there
is with it a genuine physical effort to
transcend the too-heavy burden of tragedy.

Humor and faith share the qualities of honesty and courage.

A caution is essential. Humor is more important
in dealing with our own sins than in dealing with the
pains of others. It is not for us to suggest that another person laugh away the problem brought to us. Yet,
we realize that to face the defeats of existence, the
contradictions and absurdities, with laughter can be a
high form of wisdom, and we want to face our own tragedies in this way. Such chuckling does not obscure the
dark irrationality. There is swampy ground between cyni-
cism and contrition. But the ultimate incongruities cannot be laughed away. We face them, if at all, with
faith. Humor can prepare us for faith.

Theological reflection needs humor because the
world is a perpetual caricature of itself. It is a
contradiction of what it is pretending to be. Humor is
the perception of this illusion.

OCCASIONS ON THE RUN
In our mobile society, times of movement, curi-
ously enough, may be reflective times. Driving to the
hospital for a critical call, walking to the church,
coming back from the seminary after a provocative class,
rushing on board the public transit system, flying over
the Atlantic in a plane, riding in a limousine with the
family on the way to a committal service, jogging early
in the morning -- all of these may be times we have overlooked for theological reflection.

We are not suggesting that each moment should be
put to use. We do not intend to contribute to the already frenetic pace of life which implies that each moment must be productive. Yet it is during the moments
when we are not preoccupied with tasks or planning that,
if we notice, our minds are unencumbered and the Spirit
may move in us.

OCCASIONS OF WORKING TOGETHER: Partnership
A task to be accomplished brings unusual groups

of people together in a common endeavor. Not only the public ministerial duties of community (leading worship, attending conferences, serving on committees) but also group work are thought-provoking; this might be painting a classroom, cleaning up at the church, preparing for the church auction, or sorting mimeographed reports. It is no accident that the monastic practice during the Middle Ages required the monks' physical labor to enhance their reflective discipline. Modern retreat centers often do the same.

Working together facilitates relationships and provides the opportunity for unstructured conversation in an atmosphere of mutuality. It often sufficiently diffuses energy so that differences of opinion can be heard.

> When I am busy scrubbing, your disagreement with me may be more easily accepted. A woman I know is described as "knitting very fast when controversial matters are on the floor of a meeting." Just so. Her hand activity diffuses the controversy building up and gives her time to organize her thoughts.

The ideas of partnership must become part of the ministry philosophy of the future. Individualism will not do any longer. Letty Russell speaks of the future of partnership in at least three senses.[5] First, there is the future as the basic possibility for new life-styles in marriage, friendship, church. Second, there is the future of society and the continued existence of humankind. In this sense, we must learn co-partnership, caring for one another so we do not destroy the world and ourselves. Third, there is the future that is God's. This is the eschatological hope in the purpose of life that is prefigured in the coming of Christ, and opened up by the promise and action of God.

OCCASIONS ON RETREATS
Periods of retreat are precious because they interrupt ongoing schedules, providing a break in rhythm and giving perspective. Dietrich Bonhoeffer talks about an "arcane discipline," about the value of the solitary.[6]

Retreats are open times for listening to God's Word. A quiet retreat can bring a message so loud that it cannot be denied.

> One pastor left his monastic retreat
> knowing anew that he could only love the
> people he served when he knew **himself** to
> be loved by God. The readings at meals
> had stated this loving-because-loved
> principle; it had come through the per-
> sonal reading; and it was emphasized in
> conversation with the retreat master.
> There could be no mistake God was speak-
> ing especially to him who had been busy
> doing the Lord's work without sense of
> the "everlasting arms" for himself.

A Roman Catholic priest, praying on pilgrimage
in the Church of the Annunciation in Nazareth,
said he knew God's speaking within his very
being. "You, too, as my mother, have the power
to incarnate me, by your celebration of the
eucharist and the way that you live your life
as my priest." Such a powerful experience affirmed his life call.

Life is filled with missed opportunities. The
reality of God's presence touches each element of human
existence. The occasions we have examined and illustra-
ted have been moments which can be open to God's loving
presence.

Chapter 4
A Theological Discourse
Taking One Doctrine -- Revelation -- as an Exercise
for Theological Reflection

Occasions for theological reflection are opportunities for discovering the movements of God within, not outside, the ebb and flow of human existence. To illustrate the way we work, we choose just one aspect of theology -- the Doctrine of Revelation -- for reflection. Your pensive theological moments may take you in quite different directions than ours. You will remember that we are not creating theological statements; we are ruminating on the doctrine of revelation.

REFLECTING ON PIONEERS AND PILGRIMS AS REVEALERS
We see the Christian traveler as both pilgrim and pioneer. The New Testament witnesses that the Christian life is a pilgrimage and, like all pilgrimages, it moves towards a fixed goal and along a settled path. However varied are our traditions' routes, we are agreed that the goal is the City of God and the "way" is Christ.

By itself, the image of pilgrimage could suggest that route markings have been set up and individual initiative is not encouraged. Pilgrims do not explore in the manner of pioneers. Yet Jesus, himself, is called in Hebrews 12:2 the "pioneer" of our faith, and his great missioner, Paul, certainly "pioneered" new means of proclaiming the gospel to the world and fresh understanding of his own faith.

To be a pioneer and a pilgrim at the same time is not easy, but both concepts give substance to the Christian life. They are strong and pithy. Both their strengths and defects are robust. The pilgrim who concentrates solely on the "route" will become more and more a conscientious enactor of routine and may bypass visions of beauty and human encounters which would enrich life. Such a person may have attention fixed solely on the heavenly city and tend to become the exclusive kind of ascetic or the less attractive type of puritan.

The Christian pioneer, heavily individual and

innovative, throws energy into every good work which asks for help and pursues every line of thought that seems promising. Full of enthusiasm, this pioneer, when untempered, becomes defective through a kind of "bandwagon" zest.

Such persons are the salt of the earth. Blend together this pilgrim's single-mindedness and this pioneer's imagination, and they may each see beyond their pinched goals to the Supreme Good. We are called to be both pilgrims and pioneers.

These images of pilgrim and pioneer help us to understand the relationship between theological reflection and revelation. For many persons, scripture and traditional statements of faith are, themselves, the embodiment of Christian revelation. Three approaches can be made:

1.) the pilgrim who views scripture and creed as static guides to the Kingdom,
2.) the pioneer who views them as dynamic guides for God's ongoing revelation which cannot be limited by human expression, or
3.) the pilgrim-pioneer who discovers God's message in present experience and future hope but always considers it within the context of the scriptures and a given body of faith.

The Christian who develops a habit of theological reflection becomes a pilgrim-pioneer.

REFLECTING ON NATURE AS REVELATION

We did not create ourselves. We were born of that astonishingly complex and mysterious reality that we call nature. So far as we know, humanity is nature's most highly developed product and if Jesus Christ is true humanity, he is the first clue to the creative reality at the heart of the universe.

Hostility towards nature has a utopian background. The trim garden rather than the untidy wilderness is the utopian ideal. There is the suggestion that nature must be domesticated. H. G. Wells would get rid of most animals except the cute ones. The typical utopia is a city surrounded by well-tended farmland. In C. S. Lewis' THAT HIDEOUS STRENGTH, a leader of the demonically inspired "Institute of Co-ordinated Experiments" looks forward to the day when all trees (messy and ugly things that they are, dropping leaves and pine needles) will be replaced by artificial ones more beautiful and cleaner than the original.

The name of the first utopia was Eden. Humans want to go back. We are haunted by dreams of the original garden and that lost universe. In our heart of hearts, we know that our race has not always lived in the world of historical time -- a world shot through with oppression, misunderstanding, meaningless tragedy, cruelty, individual and collective insanity -- a world only haphazardly redeemed by some deeds of niggardly virtue and grudging magnanimity and fugitive instants of compassion and love. It was not always so. Metaphysically, if not historically, it was not always so. The poor thing we commonly call our human nature was not our first nature; it is a pathological condition, we instinctively know.

We cannot reconcile ourselves to "making the best of things." For such a reconciliation is an affirmation that our exile is permanent. We are displaced persons, but our old homeland burns and glows in our hearts. If we cannot literally return to it, we can build as close a facsimile as possible. Augustine and his City of God, Calvin at Geneva, the founding fathers in New England planting their white churches in the green Canaan of the wilderness, Thomas Jefferson with his vision of the rational and benevolent society, the idealists of the French and Russian revolutions, the countless small bands of men and women in the 19th century who established co-operative communities to make Eden come true -- all these were displaced persons, pioneers trying to create a new Eden in place of the old.

REFLECTING ON KNOWLEDGE AS REVELATION
Revelation implies both a speaker and a listener, one who gives and one who receives. In Christian revelation, God is the speaker and humanity is the listener and respondent. God's work in Jesus' death and resurrection remains the primary revelation, and ongoing revelation written into the development of dogma continues the history of God's Word. Pioneering work in each era of history makes its own discoveries so that the crucified and risen Jesus throbs in each period of time, and responses to him yearn for expression in the present.

In the Hebrew Bible, all knowledge came naively; that is, one entered into it completely, and the world entered almost non-critically into the experience. For the Jew, covenant expressed the integrity of the total human experience of body and mind, individual and society, society and history.

Whether there are two types of knowledge was not a question raised by the Jews until they came into contact with the Greeks. The Greeks introduced the idea of subject and object. Objectivity gave an impersonal quality to knowledge and from that point on, history has trod a torturous path between reason and faith. It persists as a philosophical problem.

The Hebrew Bible points to the tenacious way in which the Hebrews held on to a God of history when their own history did not seem to give good reason for loyalty to the deity. Their comparatively righteous nation was destroyed. In the New Testament a righteous man was crucified. In an intense form, here are dramatizations of the question of human suffering. Will God vindicate God's chosen ones? Will God save the righteous?

No one expected the supreme meeting of God and human life to be at the Cross. Psalmists had cried for God's presence in their suffering, and prophets had contended with God in their isolation. Into such anguish the Cross came, but not the Cross only. The man, Jesus, came -- Jesus living, Jesus dying, Jesus speaking, Jesus being. The Cross came only after we had seen Jesus, and it remains the statement about human life's vulnerability and essential sadness. The Cross stabs life, but in Jesus' victory gives meaning to God's promise of life beyond suffering. Resurrection follows crucifixion.

Theological reflection mediates between the dogmatic statement which is given as Truth and ongoing experience which provides material for experiencing what is true. It mediates between belief about Jesus, the Christ, and individual apprehensions of meaning.

Karl Rahner has said that "there are many modes of creaturely mediation to the immediacy of God."[2] Humankind craves such immediacy. Current stories of faith tell us that experiences of the crucified and risen Jesus are part, too, of the reality in the twentieth century.

REFLECTING ON HISTORICAL DEVELOPMENT AND REVELATION

Most religions rest on the assertion that God communicates with humankind. Stories of the ways this self-communication has happened create the descriptive boundaries among religions. Within particular eras, place and time, availability and limitation, trial and triumph, originality and tradition have reopened peoples for new perception.

Historically, primitive humanity, fearing natural powers, ascribed to them ultimate power and named them gods. Among these gods the monotheism of Israel came out of the desert -- a land of extremes but not of violent change. The desert, to our day, creeps onto the verdant places while technology creates new oases for human habitation. Nature in the desert can be monotonous when viewed day-to-day, but its sameness is not benign; it rests precariously on the real possibility that an hour too much of sun or a cup too little of water may bring extinction.

The desert can be monotonous, yes. Was it in such a quiet uncomplicated place where God chose to reveal the real quality of life -- there steadfastly to endure facing the unity of creation, then slowly to incorporate that idea into the bustle and complexity of the city's bazaars?

From Abraham to David and on through the prophets, the Hebrews alternately declared themselves a people and despaired of being a people. At first they rested their hopes on strength and later they trusted God's favor through righteous living. Though they violated obligations and sometimes forgot their destiny, they yet confessed mistakes and called on God's leadership. They had a destiny; they lived in history. "I shall be your God and you will be my people." Even in defeat, they prayed, "The Lord our God is One."

Then Jesus was born; he taught and lived among people in their ordinariness. Into the crossroads of civilization and trade, Jesus brought a message about this human life. He sorted out the meaning of power, gave sanction to the truly committed life, and ended the questioning about political favors, the rewards of sanctity, military superiority, and social acceptance. He, an unknown and unfavored person, spoke of triumphant living and God's eternal commitment to even the least. His death spoke of the defeat of goodness, yet the certainty that he was **not** dead but lived with the All-

-Committed-One turned inside out the meanings of human reward and justification.

To make sense of this! To put it in a form for the ages! This was the task, the duty, the compulsion of the Church Fathers. They, themselves, came from various cultural milieux and the impact of a cosmopolitan world was their goad. The message was no longer a Hebrew or Palestinian word. It had to address the world. After the Fathers, the great thinkers of the Middle Ages took up the philosopher's questions of being, reality, and knowledge while at the same time maintaining the dialogue about scripture and God's relationship to the world through creation and through the special person, Jesus.

Our era has a new element. By the end of the nineteenth century, science had raised in a new voice the questions of possibility and hope, of inheritance and biological givens, of intuition and knowledge, of purpose and change.

All of this inheritance inevitably influences our reflection. We are not first century or tenth century folk. Our pilgrimage is through our own landscape and our pioneering is among our own enthusiasms; our revelations are spelled in twentieth century words. Still, the quality of revelation is ageless. It is mysterious, both surprising and eluding us. It is unprogrammable, coming at God's call. It is personal, given to each and achieving full potential only when we respond. Revelation is rendered explicit not only in Christ but in the disciples who continue the mission of Jesus.

REFLECTING ON A FEW THEOLOGIANS AND REVELATION

We can examine theological reflection through our chosen dogmatic illustration -- revelation -- if we see revelation developed by a few representative theologians. We have chosen three - John Henry Newman, Karl Barth, and Avery Dulles. Newman has influenced Roman Catholic understanding of ongoing revelation and the development of dogma. His personal faith struggle reflects a basic position in contemporary Roman Catholic understanding of revelation. Karl Barth is one representative of Protestant theology; contemporary Protestant theology must in some way respond to the critique of Karl Barth. And Roman Catholic Avery Dulles has established a typology for conceptualizing the current theology of revelation.

JOHN HENRY NEWMAN.[3]   Newman approached his study of revelation from the perspective of his own faith journey. His theory developed as he questioned whether his Anglican roots adequately expressed his experience of God's revelation. Personal experience, for Newman, included not only objects of sense perception, but also all of what it means to live out a full human existence -- relationships, intellectual activity, and personal moral dispositions.

According to Newman, experiences are apprehended in two ways: notional or real. Notional apprehension gives theology derived from abstract concepts; it results in intellectual assent. Real apprehension gives a faith derived from concrete experiences; it affects the passions, establishes principles, and forms character. Real assent in contrast to notional assent, is expressed in action. They are complementary; each leads to the other -- thought to action, and action to thought. In both, dogma and scripture are essential. In scripture revelation provides a real apprehension of the experience of God. Notional expansion conceptualizes this knowledge, always leaving to the church further development.

KARL BARTH.[4]   Karl Barth, responding to the attempt of the liberal theologians to adapt theology to science and philosophy, defended the absolute independence of God's revelation as found in the scriptures. He held that there is no general revelation at all (that is, revelation in the natural world) and that we have no knowledge of God's saving grace apart from Christ. For him, dogma, though it can never express completely the meaning of God's Word, is the human attempt to understand the implications of the scriptures for human existence. Indeed, no human expression can be Truth because the divine image in humanity has been totally obliterated by the fall. Thus, dogmatic statements are developmental expressions of humanity's attempt to understand the meaning and implications of God's Word.

If one continues Newman's usage, Barth could be thought to say that as long as truth is only notionally apprehended, it cannot lead to faith. Real apprehension must happen and it is initiated by God's call and verbalized under the inspiration of God's grace. Revelation for Barth is complete in the scriptures and there supremely in the life and death of Jesus Christ.

AVERY DULLES.[5]   In his book, MODELS OF REVELA-

TION, Avery Dulles isolates five types of revelation which encompass both Catholic and Protestant contemporary thought on a theology of revelation. Put into our words, these are the following:

1. Revelation as Doctrine.
   The Bible shows the supreme revelation of God in Jesus. The Protestant sees revelation in religious experience and in tradition, and the Catholic adds the official teaching of the church. These all become codified and are regarded as doctrine.

2. Revelation as History.
   God's self-revelation takes place in deeds; again, God's supreme deed is the vindication of Jesus at the Cross. In that historic event and in others through the intervening years, God has been revealed.

3. Revelation as Inner Experience.
   Both Protestants and Catholics consider inner experience -- defined as contemplation of the Holy, as communion, as graceful of overcoming of self -- to be revelation. Some hold that this grace is mediated by Christ alone.

4. Revelation as Dialectical Presence.
   God's revelation is, in the end, humanly imponderable. The best means for thinking about God's coming to us is to hold together the ideas of object and subject, of presence and absence, of creator, created, and spirit. What dialectic says is that no single pole adequately describes Truth, so we grasp both and reach for small apprehensions.

5. Revelation as New Awareness.
   God is not static. Humans continue finding dimensions of God's being through the insights of human activity.

Christian traditions look with shades of intensity upon their own and others' gathered ways; in other words, the denominations do not handle tradition similarly. Yet, it is through tradition that humankind preserves experiences of God's revelation. Though tradition is living and active, it contrasts with convention which is dead and passive.

> Tradition nourishes the life of the spirit; convention merely disguises its

interior decay. Tradition is creative. Always original, it opens out new horizons for an old journey. Convention, on the other hand, is completely unoriginal.[6]

Tradition takes corporate experience and makes it live. Tradition remembers. The scriptures themselves are repeated remembrances which by practice became oral tradition and later enscribed tradition. The earliest transmission of the Biblical tradition occurred around the campfire of a nomadic tribe in the Negeb. The elders told the ancient stories of the beginnings of their people -- the origins of evil, the acts of faith and courage, the beginning of law -- and this collected memory became the Bible.

Robert Moffatt in his book, THE THRILL OF TRADITION,[7] reminds us that tradition is older than Christianity. Oral tradition was the manner in which both the content and the spirit of the faith were preserved and transferred. Faith came by hearing, in the first instance.

Oral tradition has had an original and continuing role in Christian faith and nurture. Traditions can be told and retold, for generations, with astonishing fidelity to the original. Again, as Moffatt points out, literary records might be useful, but they were by no means essential for the transmission of rules, rites, and interpretations.

The Mishna (teaching by repetition) claimed to have handed down material provided by the six generations of Tannaim (that is, repeaters of tradition) between 30 B.C. and 220 A.D. To moderns unacquainted with the tenacity of the Oriental memory, it may seem almost incredible that any part of the Mishna could have been preserved for so long in memory alone. This achievement is not without other examples. The early phases of Janism in India are a parallel. Thus oral tradition both precedes the written words of scripture and serves as a vehicle for the continuing presence of the Spirit of God in the religious community.

In the Hebrew Bible itself, we find the continuing admonitions to remember the stories of God's deliverence and faithfulness. "Take heed and keep your soul diligently lest you forget the things which your eyes have seen and lest they depart from your heart all the days of your life; make them known to your children and to your children's children." Even to the present, the Jewish people have an immense sense and tradition of memory. In one sense the Jews are the rememberers for all humanity.

Remembering is what makes the Seder a great occasion. It is the burning question, "Why is this night unlike all other nights?" which opens the floodgates of memory. At the Seder the waters of history sweep over the mind, transforming the simplest and poorest room into a place of God's mighty acts. The Christian church shares with its Jewish mothers and fathers the significance of remembering. The central Christian sacrament – "This do in remembrance of Me" –– given round a table of gathered friends, draws from the passover of memory.

> Where you meet a tradition is inside the
> habits of continuous and common human
> life: in the family, the school, the
> ship and the regiment, in royal courts
> and courts of law, in colleges and par-
> liaments, and above all, in the texture
> of religious communities. Traditions
> live and move in a world of flesh and
> blood.[8]

IMPLICATIONS FOR THEOLOGICAL REFLECTION

The desire of the creature to experience the immediacy of the Creator, a theme through the ages, raises the problem of distinguishing Truth from individual hope. For Protestants the "check point" is the Bible; for Roman Catholics it is the teaching magisterium. Since even they are human constructions, the dialogue of theological reflection clarifies issues and tests tradition.

Dulles gives seven criteria in the encounter between persons who mark revelation:

1. Faithfulness to the Bible and Christian tradition.
2. Internal coherence. (It must be reasonable)
3. Plausibility.
4. Adequacy to experience (both secular and religious)
5. Practical fruitfulness (sustaining moral effort, corporate life, and mission)
6. Theoretical fruitfulness. (consistency)

7. Value for dialogue.[9]

Theological reflection, using the model applied here to the dogma of revelation, is a journey. Tradition steadies and illumines, science feeds new insight, practice tests, but the journey remains a quest without a clear end and often dimmed by doubt and conflict. In Hebrews we read, "By faith Abraham obeyed when he was called to go out to a place which he was to receive as an inheritance; and he went out, not knowing where he was to go."

Abraham was the first person who ever made a pilgrimage to the Holy Land. His life was a trek along unknown ways for God and with God. It was leisurely, too. He did not rush at full speed over the road, breathless to start a new life when he arrived. No. He lived as he went. Each stopping place was home, each overnight setdown a place for the Ark of the Covenant — holy ground. In fact, Abraham never reached his goal. He was a sojourner, a nomad, in the very land of promise — a stranger and a pilgrim everywhere.

In the Middle Ages it became the fashion in Europe to make a journey to the Holy Land. As the pilgrims came on foot down across France and Italy, traveling slowly, taking in the wonders of the lands they were visiting, people would ask where they were going. And they would reply "a la sainte terre" ("to the Holy Land"). Thus, we have the origin of the word "saunter." Saunter connoted the mood and the gait of one who found the purpose, richness, and satisfaction of life at its very best in journeying a la Sainte Terre, to the Holy Land.

In this chapter, we have spoken of revelation as one of the doctrines on which we reflect. Aspects of the doctrine have been surveyed, but in the end it is with theological reflection, itself, that we leave you — reflection on tradition and journey-taking, on pilgrims and pioneers, on Truth-seeking and revelation.

Sources of Light for our Work

What persons reflect theologically? What are
they like, those who both listen and respond to God?
Christians live in a milieu that is at least threefold
-- cultural, personal, and ecclesial.

James and Evelyn Whitehead[1] give these influences the names culture, experience, and tradition, using them as internal checks, one for the other, of the
reflection experience. They capture the aspects of human
persons in contemplation; their anthropology is ecclesial and cultural and, underneath all, personal.

Chapter 5
Anthropology: How May Christians Understand Themselves?

Human beings face both their identity and their destiny. The "Who am I?" of identity and the "What is my purpose?" of destiny are questions that intertwine; each implies the other. Who I am determines how I define purpose. As a Christian, though, I have been given a purpose; I take my self-definition at least in part from the community of faith, so I define myself against that larger mission which belongs to all Christians. Both individual and institution are joined in the work of saving and being saved.

All who believe in a Supreme Being agree in principle with the Eastern Church's understanding that humanity is only true to its nature when it knows existence is in God. But all believers do not agree about the lodging of good and evil actions; classically, this is the assignment of concupiscence, "the coveting of carnal things" (or "any inordinate devotion to a mutable good"), a quality of Christian anthropology however particularly it is defined.

In early Protestant theology, for instance, concupiscence is in the nature of every person, rendering her/him sinful (i.e. fallen), though the individual doer of a sinful deed is justified by faith in God's forgiving grace. In this view, pride and self-interest always taint a good act; none can be pure. More radical reformation believers say that this outlook despairs of the God-given goodness in humanity, and they prefer to emphasize striving towards goodness as an actual possiblity. Catholic theologians view concupiscence as a result of the loss of primitive nature and not as sin.

In spite of these differences, all Christians agree that God wills salvation for all. Each person's obligation is to be receptive to God's self-communication. Women and men are loved by God who wills their companionship, indeed ultimate residence, with the One who loves them. But having been created into freedom, they can say "yes" or "no" to this divine offer. And personal experience illustrates that there is, in fact, struggle between each one's temporal desires and human yearnings for all-rightness with the Eternal, of unity with God.[1] In all, we are self-conscious, knowing well both sides of our dual nature. ".....we are separated from the unity that is of our nature and subjected to a remorseless and inescapable duality. By nature we are a part of nature. By nature we are apart from nature."[2]

In Masefield's long poem, "The Widow in the Bye Street," we hear the echo all Christians would affirm -- that those who come to God are already known, that grace is available for all. A brokenhearted mother is making a last prayer for her son who is to be executed for murder. She prays,

> And God who gave his mercies,
>   takes his mercies.
> And God who gives beginning,
>   gives the end.
> A rest for broken things
>   too broke to mend.[3]

Life has many broken things "too broke to mend" --diseases from which one cannot recover, losses which one can never forget, disappointments too great to be passed over, failures too complete ever to be made right. The Gospel proclaims that all broken things are still in the hands of the Mender of broken things. God is still God of all. The vision awaits its time.

Benedict, the founder of western monasticism, describes prayer as "the unrestricted admittance of the divine into human life, even at the price of alternative self-gratification and apparent independence."[4] Humanity must constantly struggle with concupiscence which often comes between God's voice and genuine human listening. Monastic practices of the Middle Ages helped individuals to free themselves from world preoccupations and allowed the monks to give full attention to discerning God's Word. In contemporary society, we look for ways of life which allow us, too, to hear how we should act and, when the fragility of age or disease has taken us beyond the ability to do, to know at least how we should be.

Adrian van Kaam,[5] who initiated the new religious discipline of formative foundational spirituality, assumes that each person is present to the Divine. Because of the human disposition to self-centeredness and sin, there are various levels of existence, i.e., ways of knowing God's presence. Van Kaam develops four ways: biosensual, functional, romantic, and existential commitment -- each having spiritual and psychological dimensions. They are given here with our own development.

a. The Biosensual Level:
Following psychological developmental theory,
we know that the human infant requires fulfillment of the fundamental needs for physical comfort, food, and closeness. All these hungers
have physical means of satisfaction (dryness
and warmth, milk, and touch) and psychological
means of satisfaction (tactile ease, satiety,
and unaloneness). As the child develops and is
able to extend awareness beyond the body, giving reality to other aspects of life, he or she
begins to "know" the outer and inner worlds as
distinct.   It is clear that "good enough" nurturing of the earliest self-centered needs is
an essential ground for the attainment of further broader development.
b. The Functional Level:
Still primarily self-centered, but now also relating to the outer world, the person is at
work towards ego mastery, experienced as a desire for control, for having and possessing.
Having discovered that satisfiers of needs
(clothes, food, mother) are not extensions of
self but belong to a world ever so slightly removed from self, the person has to find ways to
command that world of fulfillment. This extends
for a long time -- for many, into maturity.
Even the object of prayer at this level is experienced as self-improvement. Moral control is
understood self-righteously. Friendship plumps
up self-importance. Comfort of the individual
is still a primary concern.
c . The Romantic Level:
There is movement from the self towards another
-- not the world in general but specific others. Our relationships are not only conquests;
they mean something to us. The words "satisfaction" and "fulfillment" gain depth. Relating to
others and to The Other has affective rewards
for us. Feelings of belonging and care are
sought, not alone in human friendship but in
religious communion.
d . The Level of Existential Commitment:
With maturation come clearer notions of goals
and more realistic assessment of the possible.
We ask how we shall live when the idea of complete control is discovered to be wishful
thinking, a child's dream, and when the world's
offerings no longer fully satisfy. Human life
is partial, we know, yet commitment to the

49

Person-Who-Beckons is a poignant choice. Tied as we are to the world with all its unGodlike parts, existentially committed, our surrender to God is not complete. We play the game of giving up self in mature acceptance of mission yet continuing to nurture -- sometimes outrageously -- our human needs.

Persons will act on all levels at once, even to the ends of our lives. Of course. We are by nature in this world, a part of it; we are by nature aware of our apartness. At one time we continue to be the babied individual in search of physical and psychological gratification. At other times we function, even religiously, as though we have found the world but want to bring it into ourselves, for ourselves alone. We move toward others in reckless enjoyment of the affective satisfactions and still want to surrender ourselves for the "beingness" of belonging to creation, itself. We accept mission for its community and for its ideal. We want both to know ourselves in rich luxurience of experience and to give ourselves in full surrender to an ideal. One can call these conflictual experiences, or one can call them the ambivalences of the Christian anthropology.

In theological reflection, our choices and stumbling blocks are brought to the fore, and we give expression to facets of our lives we had not before acknowledged. Accepting that we are infantile and mature in almost the same moment, we learn to love both ourselves and the world with new devotion.

Read in one way, all this sounds like a self-improvement bulletin. It is the trap of the development chart. Progression among levels of awareness looks much like a ladder to God. What nonsense! The mysterious, illusive, interesting Carer whom we love is brought before us in the figure of Jesus and removed from the dimension of effort into the dimension of relation. We are given to each other, not won. In Him we have set before us not a program but a life -- not an achievement scheme, but a quality -- and the quality to which Jesus points has something of the essence of ecstatic reason (a term of Paul Tillich).[6] In our human anthropology, we attempt understanding through reason, but Christians can reap an ecstatic understanding not "unreasonable" but reasonable in its depths ..... to the place of the ultimate. Tillich says "ecstatic reason is reason overpowered, invaded, shaken by ultimate concern."

Personal holiness can be expressed as "me-ism", the dark side of human potential. Excessive self-concern, even holy desire, makes of conceit and pride a sin. Not to recognize the appeal and deep roots of self-preservation to the point of sickness invites another kind of decay, a decay expressed as too much sweetness. We too easily speak of the beauties of community without paying attention to the soft and careless qualities of life together. The predilection for me-centeredness is so universal that we begin to achieve true fellowship only when we acknowledge how hard it is to love and to care. Then -- and then, alone -- do our goals aim to maintain justice. Justice, not soft fellowship, Reinhold Neibuhr reminded us, has to come first in a society which cannot get far away from self-interest and individual gratification.

Niebuhr's word was in the context of "moral man, immoral society."[7] It is possible to pursue "good" goals, to live nice lives, to enjoy faithful relationships even while the world slides away in unconcern, oppression, brutality, or war. Personal love and care do not provide strong community necessarily. Emphasis on justice with its calculating balance of requirements gives structural strength; like the wire mesh embedded into concrete foundations, justice maintains square and dependable dimensions.

Architects work from the perspective of the next larger context. The room has to be seen in the context of the house, the house in the context of the site, the site in the context of the area's ecology. So our self-concerns must be seen in the next larger context, ultimately God's context, because this makes of our concerns ethical considerations.

Life keeps putting the ethical question. Hour by hour, ego wants to be in the way of humanity, wants to say, "Satisfy me first." Looking at life, though, from the next larger context lifts ego ever so slowly away from itself.

The hearer of God's Word -- sinner and healed -- who always stands in God's graceful space lives in a larger context which influences the nature of a concrete response to the Divine invitation. The next larger context of our Christian anthropology may be called conture.

Chapter 6
Culture

Of the many dictionary definitions for culture, most have to do with agriculture, to the cultivation of the soil. Extended to the field of learning, we speak of a cultivated person as one who has refinement, breeding, or polish. Growth is implied, even assumed, but it is the tending that defines culture's health and quality.

As we use it, the cultivation of a Christian life gives the idea of growth in faith, defined by reverence and value. As the farmer cultivates the plants, the Christian cherishes life itself -- giving value to every breathing thing because it has first been cherished by God.

We care about every single creation and how it is used. Though the words "culture" and "civilization" have at times been used interchangeably, the latter has taken on the attributes of manipulative accomplishment, of accumulated possession, of the acquisition of "better things" -- some of them known as culture. In short, civilization clearly speaks of devices, mechanisms, techniques, and instrumentalities by means of which we live. Culture is more subtle, pointing towards the expression of life's meaning through the release of artistic energy. In culture we think of cooperation with the qualities inherent in each one, and we think of regard for one another heightened by the nuances of difference.

Civilization is useful; it gets us something needed or wanted. It is utilitarian. Culture, we have to admit, has been used historically as a measurement for oppression (think of the cultural groups who defended their values through the ways of war and cruelty) and sociologically as a tool for valuing populations (think of the cultural "standards" which have lent strength to putting into segregated places those who do not meet the qualifications of the measuring group). But these are its underside -- the evidences of concupiscence. What culture means to be is an amalgam of values, at their best able to qualify the kind of civilization they elicit.

We use civilization, and it is easily handed down. Contrivances invented in one generation are taken for granted in the next. They are improved, expanded, and soon become definers of a style of living. But a profound culture is not so. It must be experienced by every person -- its insights and devotions individually reproduced, its values inwardly possessed and assimilated. No one can, on another's behalf, love Bach's "O Sacred Head Now Wounded." There are no proxies for the soul. No one else can do our living for us.

Civilization is easily transmissible, not only vertically from parents to children (cars, T.V., computers, and electric fry pans) but horizontally (from nation to nation, continent to continent). Start using a contrivance anywhere and in the long run it will be everywhere. The inventive spirit is unquenchable and unless regulated by consensus, the genius -- benign or diabolical -- will erupt. But the profound faiths that give life meaning, the moral ends to which this vast agglomeration of mighty implements will be devoted -- the spiritual culture -- have no such swiftness of transference.

Barbara W. Hargrove wrote,
Analysis of present day culture reveals that we are immersed in the mire of bureaucracy and technology. The self-worth of the individual is equated with professionalism. As a result a "new class" has emerged. This class is not founded on wealth or social status but upon knowledge. The prevailing theme is equality.[1]

Caught up in this heady bit of accomplishment which brings comfort as well as acclaim, most people can see no further than the civilized effects of things and fulfillment. But social scientists, on the other hand, refer to the nurturing, feeding, shaping effects of culture and say that one of culture's functions is to make up for deficiencies in private wisdom. It allows us to know with our feelings what we do not, by philosophical standards, know with our minds. Culture has the power to redeem civilization.

We are children of an age come to a cultural no-exit road. Dachau and Hiroshima ended the age, even though there are still persons who wander around in a cul-de-sac at the end of the road. In this age just past, we gained confidence in the categories of experience that are rational, objective, and demonstrable. It allowed us to think that to know Jesus we had only to examine the records through every discipline academia offers, and we would have a "reasonable" knowledge of him. Religion, like civilization, was quantified, studied, and applied, much as though it were a journey into entrepreneurship.

> Little by little, we substract
> Myth and fallacy from fact,
> The illusory from the true;
> And starve on the residue.[2]

Another way of making the comparison between civilization and culture is to face, as we do in our generation, the laws of consequence. Pollution, critical shortages, hunger, over-population haunt us. Robert Louis Stevenson once said that sooner or later we all sit down to a banquet of consequences. The banquet is part of our daily judgment. We have to eat; we have an option in what we shall eat and our only possible choices are what is set before us. Look at what civilization has offered us -- fear of disease and malnourishment even in the wellfed parts of the earth, because civilization's relentless momentum has invented "nutrition" which may yet poison our bodies. The Lord may prepare a table before us in the presence of our enemies but the banquet of consequences is provided from our own larder and may not be so pleasant. It often becomes more nearly "the bread that each one eats alone."

Culture is the cultivation of those values which transcend, judge, and redeem time. Culture transcends political systems; look at Rome's utter destruction of Greece as a world power -- on the battlefield, on the sea, in the marketplace, and at the council table -- and then remember also that after all the work of ruin and rot and pillage was accomplished and Greece had been reduced to ashes, no Roman would be called cultivated unless Greek was spoken and conversation had its life in Greek culture. When Vandal and Goth had similarly disposed of Rome and wolves wandered among the ruins of the Forum, across the northern marshes of the Adriatic a new civilization was soon to flower based on the Greek understanding of art and architecture, drama and poetry.

Culture as cultivation of reverence toward life's possibilities does not avoid learning; Christians do not turn back the knowledge clock. Culture, though, accepts and adopts learning's accomplishments, sifting their applicability. Each person responds to culture as ability, training, and sensitivity advise. During the hours of theological reflection, we test our ability and discover our sensitivity so that our responses to culture are those we, ourselves, can tune.

Consider two men of World War II, both in Germany, both confronted by nearly the same circumstances. In the foreward of a book entitled PAUL SCHNEIDER, THE PASTOR OF BUCHENWALD, E. H. Robertson writes,

> Paul Schneider was a simple German pastor of the Reformed tradition. He was not brilliant and would probably never have been known outside the small circle of his friends if his integrity had not been tried on a national scale.....Many more brilliant men found reasons for cooperating with the Nazis. Paul Schneider could not thus betray himself.....We read the record of a man who fought Naziism for no other reason than that he could not disobey Christ.[3]

Schneider had not looked on the long range meaning of political reality; he was not a participant in a movement. The issue came for him in his daily round of work as preacher and pastor. Because of his stand against the interference of the state with the work of the church, his church, he was banished to another area and warned not to preach. Several times he refused and came back to his parish. Finally he was arrested and sent to Buchenwald from which he never returned.

Schneider's act was different from Dietrich Bonhoeffer's. Bonhoeffer became involved in political opposition; he organized his own seminary; he was a national figure. Schneider was an unobtrusive country parson who protested when the state interfered with the church's freedom. He would probably not have described his brave stand as a "cause," but he was an honest follower of the right as he interpreted it. His response to culture was in the spirit of his own ability and training -- small in arena, quiet in tone, adamant in conviction. Bonhoeffer's growing years were nurtured in financial comfort, educational superiority, and artistic accomplishment,[4] so one can suppose that this gave him the range of thought and imaginative conceptualizing of the future which put him to work among the leaders of his age. But both men died in prison camp -- and for the same belief.

After the War, Joseph Pieper in LEISURE: THE BASIS OF CULTURE said that culture depends for its very existence on leisure, and leisure in its turn is not possible unless it has a durable and consequently living link with the cultus, with divine worship. This is the usage we have pursued.

> .....it is of the first importance to see that cultus, now as in the distant past, is the primary source of man's freedom and independence within society. Suppress that last sphere of freedom and freedom itself and all our liberties will in the end vanish into thin air.[5]

Chapter 7
Ecclesiology

The Christian community organized as church is the artistic material calling forth theological and spiritual maturity. There is a givenness within its boundaries -- "given" time, "given" space, "given" opportunities, "given" crises. All these derive their perimeters from the larger borders of life, itself. Inside their bounds lies the possibility to sense the meaning of grace for pondering and coping with the givens of the life each of us knows.

The church is strong because it points beyond itself. When there is true graciousness, the church unmeasuringly embraces all of life. But graciousness can be blunt, when it means to be gracious not towards some but in justice towards all. The church is indeed blunt (one could say realistic) in the message of limits, those limits which no amount of love or "right thinking" can erase. Accident, disease, devastating disappointment, death are not negotiable events in life; they respond to no gracious overturning.

In the face of movements that would wash all meaning from words like pain, brokenness, and evil by asserting that love can conquer, the church must continue asserting that human life is creaturely; it has limits. All unfolding and enterprise, in fact all faith and development, all moral vision and achievement, are realized within limited time. Indeed, they achieve urgency from the limits. And they are susceptible to the gracious intervention of understanding and strength.

But conceived as a fellowship in which both human teaching and divine revelation can occur, the Holy Spirit has been so "tracked" in the organized church that even spirituality is thought to depend upon the formation given by directors and modes of worship. Living in the spirit, though, occurs neither by order nor necessarily by passivity. Where Christians are together, growth happens in relationship to the environment, depending upon the nourishment there provided.

In fish biology, the same principle applies. It is called the auto-catalytic principle. That is, a fish will grow to the size supportable by the amount and nu-

59

tritive value of the water in its habitat. Thus, small
fish -- little goldfish, for instance -- live in small
fish bowls. The same goldfish would have grown into
large carp if they had been released into a pond or river; in some states goldfish have been banned as bait because those that escape become huge carp that roil the
water with mud as they forage for plant food. Since fish
live in large groups, though not necessarily in schools,
they further adjust their growth in relation to their
numbers. Thousands of experiments have proved that each
pond has a specific poundage of fish that it can support
(either a lot of small fish totaling that poundage or
several large ones).

(The sunfishes, particularly, have caused mam-
moth problems. They produce prolifically and are peculiarly prone toward dwarfing. Without predators to thin
the population, sunfish become more and more numerous --
and begin maturing at smaller and smaller sizes. Finally, the pond is filled with tiny fish that are mature,
reproducing and growing so slowly that in practical
terms they are not growing at all. Sport clubs once
viewed such ponds as "fished out" and dumped in more
fish for catching. But they compounded the catastrophe.)

This illustration is not an analogy; the church
cannot be likened either to the pond or to the fish population. But it is a point (parable?) for theological
reflection, because there are similarities, and the
pond/fish idea presents questions for Christians. Protestants and Catholics agree that the believing community is a permanent presence of God's self-disclosure to
the world. Like the physical body, though, the Body of
Christ as church changes through reclamation, replace-
ment, and reflection. That is, as a person's body is
reclaimed by healthful activity, replaced by cell death
and division, and changed by thoughtful intent, yet it
is still the same body, so the church is changed yet the
same from age to age.

The church fellowship has all the qualities of a
stream that can be either supportive or fished out. God
loves each person, placing him or her among peers and
nurturers. In theological reflection we pick out the
characteristics of healthy support and examine the qualities that encourage persons to know themselves as God's
children.

Ecclesia, though, is more than a "put and take"
operation. Though the fish bowl illustration is sugges-

tive and, indeed, cautionary, it leaves out just those qualities we have been urging. It does not approach the qualities of tenderness, unknown-ness (mystery), fresh-given awareness (revelation, expectancy of change, hope) and the pain of waiting (failure).

The auto-catalytic environment of a fish pond is a bargain struck with nature. Much human day-to-day routine is kept sane and possible by just such organizational understanding of the human community, but what makes of the church a gathering of the faithful, ecclesia, is the sensibility that unnamed communication and response point beyond mere accommodation towards the welcoming arms of "home." The community of believers proclaims this message in at least three ways: in koinonia, diakonia, and martyria.

Koinonia suggests the kind of fellowship in which the community of believers gives witness by its way of living together -- the members being willing to sacrifice themselves for the common good. Compelled by Jesus' willing acceptance of death on a cross, Christians look to koinonia in support of their own struggle to empty themselves of self-concern and gain atonement.

Diakonia reflects Christ's service by continuing the care of humankind. Wanting all of humanity to experience God's love temporally and eternally, Christians give active service to their neighbors. In such ministry the church gives both hint and promise of God's kingdom as Jesus promised.

Martyria is seen in willingness to give up life itself for the faith. Somehow Christians are called to give witness to faith's reality. Living as Jesus taught is a life-long set of adjustments in which contemporary events are faced, each in turn, with reflective desire and tenacity. We know that such witness-living can bring heavy consequences in personal status, financial benefits, and social acceptance -- "reversal" is the word the world would use to describe what happens to those who adjust their material circumstances by their interpretation of Jesus' injunctions.

In each era, the church responds anew to proclamation. In ours, koinonia's shaping has looked at church authority. In the Catholic church we seek the meaning of collaboration. In Latin America and other places, basic communities are trying to become koinonia.[1] In denominations, the issues of peace and social justice span first and third world communities; in the beginning international efforts are often like diakonia, taking good things from the first world to the third, but afterwards they begin to act as fellowship (koinonia) to **share** the work and fruits of concern. In directed spirituality, we may be seeing efforts toward developing inner resources which enable martyria.

There is a concept which is very old in the history of theology -- the church visible and the church invisible. The church visible is the structure, the building with its committees, program, projects, and personnel. It is the church visible which gives evidence of the divisions in the many denominations. But the church invisible is wherever there is grace and compassion, forgiveness and openness -- the characteristics of our Lord Jesus.

Our hope becomes real only when it is shared. It is not selfish hope. Jesus was always listening to and lifting up the burdens of people. It is through such activity of the church invisible that humanity can find a reason for existence in spite of the absurdities of cancer, the threat of nuclear holocaust, starvation, and the systemic evils with which humankind struggles. This is why the church is. The invisible church supplies Christ-like possibilities, but the visible church takes on those possibilities, not inadvertantly but as one called.

> We make ourselves a place apart
>   Behind light words that tease and flout
> But oh, the agitated heart
>   Till someone finds us really out.
>
> 'Tis pity if the case require
>   (or so we say) that in the end
> We speak the literal to inspire
>   The understanding of a friend.
>
> But so with all, from babes that play
>   At hide-and-seek to God afar
> So all who hide too well away
>   Must speak and tell us who they are.[2]
>   .....Robert Frost

In the church we tell each other who we are, really -- assuming we can trust one another to share hopes, fears, dreams, and angers -- and we meet the Divine Offerer of love, strength, courage, and meaning.

The Bible is a human record of divine revelation. In the fertility of its accounting, it covers the ground of human experience and its implications are forever evolving. This is the work not only of systematic and exegetical study but also of rumination and worship. Theological reflection takes the studies and, with an admixture of appreciation/analysis, thinks about the infusion of religion into life.

Holding the mission to make into a continual reality the revelation of God in Jesus, the church is both institution and a gathering of individuals. Through the latter who can express unconditional love of their neighbors, there is the taste of God's unchanging love. Inside the church the love of God in Jesus is ritualized and sacramentalized; its urgent reaching for the beauty of all beauties, the fleshliness of every embodiment, the tenderness of eternal care, the starkness of absolute justice is a grasp for what is true. In each effort the yearning is known to be universal and the repeated sign in art and behavior has become sacramental. In theological reflection we look at the inspired record and God's continuing self-communication.

Chapter 8
The Bible and Theological Reflection

Uniquely central in Christian tradition, the Bible gives an experiential record of some of God's intervention in history. On the weight given to the Biblical authority and the ways in which the writing has been inspired, denominations differ, but all Christians say at least that the scriptures have been given by the leading of the Holy Spirit. All subsequent reflections upon God's part in historical development must take into account the early telling. The canon is given to us as fundamental. New insights in dogmatic teaching or the church's activity are included as implied in scripture through the "sensus plenior" (the full sense).

For Catholic Christians, conclusions and insights leading to actions and teachings must be seen as part of the "sensus plenior" of the scriptures; thus, the work of "seeing" in this way is the work of theological reflection. But other Christians, though they may not be expected to refer to this discipline, do hold to a self-imposed requirement of testing further queries by the earliest documents; to "stay within the faith" has in some way to do with respect and discretion in regard to the scriptures.

Referring to the full sense of the scriptures is quite a different matter than interpreting the scriptures. By the wildest stretch of the imagination, theological reflection could be expected to be able to accommodate most thinking under the rubric of an interpretation. But theological reflection does not intend to "fit" current practice into biblical modes. Theological reflection is more accurately described as the wrestling ground on which the contention between inclination and practice is brought into scrutiny under the light of biblical criticism and interpretation. Under no circumstances does the reflector put aside the academic disciplines, for they are the substance with which the reflection is done.

Jan H. Walgrave says, "If, then, a definite truth, determined by God, has to be preserved in the presence of divergent interpretations, the idea of an institutional authority, equally determined by God and enabled by Him to settle controversies of interpretation, is as natural to the mind as the idea of an historically revealed truth itself."[1] This is helpful in churches who seek an authoritative finality.

What is happening for some Protestants is, however, quite different. Often precipitated by movements that have joined strands of Protestant expression, there is frequently an agonizing effort to hold together two important threads:

     1.) the biblical tradition, however variously interpreted, which must remain the root "raison d'etre" and

     2.) the divergent traditional dogma which must, without becoming minimalist, enrich rather than entangle the emerging document.

For these Protestants, the boundaries of the "sensus plenior" are sufficient; for those who accept the reality of magesterial authority, institutional authority is a guardian of revelation and must be considered a perimeter as well.

For our purposes, in illustration, we isolate five biblical forms of faith discussion.

> **The narrative discourses** (Abraham's story, Exodus, the Gospels' life of Jesus)
> **The prescriptive discourses** in which God speaks as through norms (the law of Moses, the new commandment of love)
> **The prophetic discourses** which challenge, censure, and lead to response (all of the prophets)
> **The wisdom discourses** which raise basic questions of human existence (suffering in the book of Job)
> **The hymnic discourses** giving humanity's response to God through praise and petition (the Psalms)[2]

(Karl Rahner makes the point that the canon brings together every kind of spiritual experience, and it must have been the council's intent that within this selection of books there should be included these testimonies of God's presence. Together they are God's word in all its unfolding.

Protestants can learn from Catholics the strength of the boundaries of testimony. Boundaries do not only limit; they also include, and this is what Protestants often miss. When a bounded selectivity such as the canon is provided for us within the church's teachings, there is the opportunity/responsibility that we check our perceptions against all the testimonies -- not only the one which best fits our perceptions. In this instance, the boundary opens out the possibilities instead of restricting them.)

We as part of the historical context continue these discourses, using our own stories as part of the theological reflection process. In our narratives, as well as the biblical ones, is the discovery of God's presence. We, too, pick up the mood of scriptural prescriptions and make current ones based on conditions of life now changed mostly by technology. Churches provide standards; political action groups do, too; and so do humanitarian interest groups. Our society also has its prophets -- religious, social, political, artistic -- who, following the leading of their gods, proclaim systemic changes in human organization.

Peoples' experience of suffering and death, misery and hopelessness, make concrete the paschal mystery of the life-giving death in the heart of Christian faith. The "why" questions are ongoing wisdom discourses.

Prayer and worship incorporating twentieth century forms respond to our need to voice praise and petition in our own vocabulary and reality.

Commentaries and perceptive appreciation of history's movement with God into the present cannot take the place of the Bible, itself, as source for theological reflection. Thus, we are not biblical students so much as we are empathizers trying to sense our way into another way of life and thought that is not naturally our way. (The parabolic mood)

> is the mood of one whose heart is chilled and whose spirit is saddened by a sense of loneliness, and who, retiring within himself, by a process of reflection frames thought-forms which half conceal, half reveal (these moods) -- reveal them more perfectly to those who understand, hide them from those who do not -- forms beautiful, but also melancholy as the hues of the forest in late autumn.[3]

Dr. Eugene Wehrli points out that the Kingdom of God is central in Jesus' teaching.[4] It, too, is a thought-form not designating a place or future life or visible church. Rather it designates God's rule. In Greek, the noun "kingdom" is formed from a verb -- therefore carrying with it more the idea of action than do our English words "king" or kingdom." These latter are static, suggesting things or places or persons. We do not say "to king," but we do have a comparable usage "to rule." This activity is closer to our experience and if we regard feminist concerns for the suggestibility of our language use, we will see that "rule" and its close kinship to "sovereignty" carries fewer overtones of male overlordship. Kings and lords are never, by definition, women. But sovereigns have been, in biblical times and in ours, female persons. Where God is sovereign, God's time has come.

When we deal with the Bible directly, we must encounter not only interpretations, but as we are looking at it here, ways of thinking and being. Matthew's use of the term, "kingdom of heaven," reminds us again of the Jews' restraint about calling God by name. We are struck by the urgency with which the Gospel writers needed to demonstrate how different from all they had known was Jesus' message. It is different from all that we know, too, and we struggle with understanding whether the outrageous story lines and conclusions are meant to be prescriptions for behavior or indications of the overturned priorities Jesus wanted us to understand about God. Parable after parable presents us with this continuing dilemma: shall I read this to tell me how, specifically, to live or shall I glimpse Jesus in the throes of urging me to rethink "natural" responses to friend or foe, neighbor or stranger?

In the Bible we meet people who are unlike us (though perhaps not so unlike others in our world whom we do not understand any better than we do Biblical folk; how western we are is all-too-apparent in cross-cultural greeting). The encounter of the strange is a religious experience for it requires of us humility, regard, and in the end embrace if we are to be enriched -- and, indeed, if we are to acknowledge as God's creation all of the created world and not only that part we know and love.

When our compassion and mutual employ-
ment are accompanied by the development
of awe, respect, and vision, our pride

of seeing others as only like ourselves
is replaced by our humility of realizing
that others see us as strange......Wel-
coming strangers involves entering into
the conditions of loneliness, solitude,
and companionship.....Welcoming strangers involves increasing forays into the
realms of friendships, encountering new
individuals, new groups....., new representatives of the generations......Look-
ing at each other, and at all others
both amazed and amused, we give and receive life.[5]
Isn't this what scripture as paradigm of life does for
us?

From this reality and joy, pastoral work in ritual and at bedside, in groups of old and young, is the
development of trust in the Holy Spirit. Each can have
hope as a persistent trust in the sacred experience of
others seen in the Bible and in our surrounding life. We
may find in the renewed study of scriptures and church
history that some of the ancient religious vocabulary
has a patina, a depth of association, an accumulated
force and mystery which is peculiarly apt.

In Karl Rahner's words:
The Spirit in the sense meant here.....
occurs always and everywhere in the life
of someone who has awakened to personal
self-possession and to the act of freedom in which he disposes of himself as a
whole. But in most cases in human life,
this does not come about expressly in
meditation, in experiences of absorp-
tion, etc., but in the material of normal life -- that is, when responsibility, fidelity, love, etc. are realized
absolutely.....[6]

Reflecting on the Bible brings us to think about
the Christ, not alone the Jesus of Palestine. We look at
Christ as God in concreteness -- enjoying the routine of
a carpenter's family, the rugged pleasure of the fisher-
man's life, the solitude of the open sea, or the arduous
climb of a steep ascent. In Christ we meet God enduring
commonplace bigotry, smug authority, or personal self-
righteousness. Thus, our Christology presents us with
deity not alone as sovereign but as suffering servant.
It is in the ordinary more than the extraordinary that

we discover God's spirit.

In Pompeii the guide shows the remains of the theater in which only comedies were played and then alongside it those where only tragedies were presented. But life offers, unseparated, comedy and tragedy flowing together in amazing confusion. Theological reflection faces into this ambiguity.

Chapter 9
Sacrament and Theological Reflection

One aspect of theological reflection is intellectual exercise, a stimulus that can be either self-serving or missional. The first tends to die in the self while the latter moves outwards in growth and service. Still, we cannot denigrate entirely the pleasure of thinking out faith and its relationships. If belief is to eventuate in joyful service, it ought to have a quality of satisfaction; it is only when that glow of intellectual congruence becomes its own end that theological reflection is idolatrous. As a beginning, though, there is great invitation to life in Christ when two persons come together both to examine and reflect upon faith.

It is the Divine Revealer who is at work with us in the mentoring relationship and when we are aware of that Presence and look for the symbolism of being and act in our own surroundings, we are leaving the pure study of faith and entering the holy arena of sacrament. Such signs of the holy cast upon our work the shadow of beckoning as in an open doorway, the shadow of mystery as in a darkened profile, and the shadow of possibility as in a sun or moonlit path on water.

Sign and symbol are not the same. In one respect they are similar; they both point beyond themselves to something else. The typical sign, for instance the red light at street corners, does not point to itself but to the necessity of stopping. A symbol points beyond in a metaphorical way; it somehow suggests what is to come, yet does not "mean" what is beyond. One could say that a sign has a limited meaning which has come to be associated with it -- as "red" with "stop." But a symbol has limitless meaning and it has ceased to be symbolic if meaning has been locked into it and dogmatized. Signs are shortcuts to meaning. Symbols are excursions into meaning.

Another way to say this is that signs do not in any way participate in the reality and power of that to which they point. Symbols, although not the same as that which they symbolize, do participate in its meaning and power. The letters "A" and "R" do not participate in the sound to which they point. They are signs. A flag does participate, evoking strong feelings for the power and security of the nation. It is a symbol.[1]

We create our own symbols. Sometimes they give form to an aspect of awareness which is happening inside us. A seagull's cry may, to an ecologist mean a dirty bird's carrying junk into the pond, but for me personally (even though I, too, care about the pond and know the reality of ecology's message) that cry symbolizes the sea's vastness,

.....unknown possibilities,
..... nearness to creation's edge,
.....aching beauty not in the
bird, itself, but in the
beauty I associate with
the seaworld around the
bird.

Even when I hear the gull's cry on TV in an inane commercial, it evokes in me those same feelings.

Such a symbol can remain symbolic for just me, one person, but the reality is that most such experiences when shared are found to resonate with someone else's experience. Then they bring meaning of a greater magnitude. On such reception by a larger group hinge great events of history, because the group decides to be together in order to share the expanded resonation.

All great leaders know this, and many create symbols and group response for their own benefit. Mob psychology or hysteria has been an important aspect of every historical movement. Religious persons use criteria to measure whether a symbol and its attenuating events are good and proper (righteous) or wrong and unfair (sinful). Catholics have the magesterium to keep the congregation's response within the bounds of accepted symbolism and expected mission. Protestants evaluate against the "Protestant Principle" as Tillich called it, asking always whether the response serves the greater purposes of God and the common good of the community.

We Christians call the aweful moments of congruence between symbol and meaning, between symbol and act, times of grace. They are Godgiven insights upon which we build a larger vision. They have the power to grant worth and to judge both historical times and contemporary achievement, thus allowing our design of the earthly kingdom and our apprehension of God's sovereignty to be composed not alone of past discernments but of present intuitions.

Sacraments reach even beyond the notions of sign or symbol. They not only participate in that for which they stand; they actualize the reality and power to which they point. The continued reality of God's revelation in Jesus Christ is actualized in sacrament by the churches in the activity of its members. We are actualizations of God's meaning when we take our lives to be sacramental, wholly given to God's use.

And we are God's questions to ourselves and our world. Just when are we, in fact, living sacramentally? To whom do we point for illustration: to "accomplishment" in the mission field? to lives given up to death in oppressive places? to service lovingly and fatefully given to the poor and sick? to councils of Christians working for peace and justice? Can it be that the "mustard seeds" of sacramentality are around us in suburb and campus, on pavement and field, in cleanliness and filth? These are the agonizings we bring into theological reflection -- reflection that never ends, because these are the questions we never answer for all time.

If this is a moral universe, it is not so obviously moral that a person is likely to discern the morality singlehandedly anymore than one would be likely to stumble onto the laws of physics. Dr. Huston Smith[2] suggests that this parallel is instructive. From a reasonable, clear-eyed observation of the moral scene, one would be likely to conclude almost nothing. But let a person get hold of a postulate, and it becomes a different matter.

According to Webster's dictionary, a postulate is "a hypothesis advanced as an essential presupposition, condition or premise of a train of reasoning." In Christianity we have a living postulate, sacramentalized for us in the church.

Let one get hold of a postulate tied to a person and that one can be led to conviction. Let one work life into a postulate as, for instance, "He that loseth his life for my sake shall find it" and by worldly standards this would seem an unlikely truth. But a cloud of witnesses will tell you that most of life does confirm such a postulate. Not all of life, however. As the Epistle to the Hebrews puts it, "As it is, we do not see everything in subjection to Him, but we see Jesus."

We have had a living postulate. And we can be
living postulates, ourselves. We have had Jesus, and we
can follow him. There is exultation in that. We can and
must become sacraments of our living postulate.

Theological reflection without response in the
form of sacrament is like artistry without the media to
take idea to form. It is an exercise in futility --
lacking excitement, enthusiasm, or accomplishment. With
reflection to guide symbolism, the sacraments we have
been given and those we create become fulfillments of
faith in action.

Second Part: THE CONTEXT

Section I
People - the Artists

Practitioners of every discipline try to make themselves clear through examining the process by which they work and making it into a system. Even the "pure" arts, after the thrill of first discovery, refine their encounter into teachable steps. Only a few "primitives" remain, artists who want deliberately to avoid structure. Yet one suspects that even they have come to some conclusions about the media and method that best suit their purposes of being unclaimed by a school of art.

Very young children sometimes sit at the piano and play what they have heard -- even an amazingly intricate piece of music. Or they play lines they, themselves, have created. We marvel at the hearing, pitch, and facility of mind that can do this without training, and for a while we try not to touch this awesome creativity. But, eventually, if the child does not give up, a person takes hold of this ability and tries to shape it, realizing what a world of possibility is available to a person with such a sense of music.

So when we call theological reflection an art, we resist systematizing it. Religion, itself, is an art which has suffered inside the systems laid upon it in the name of insight and regularizing. The religious experience in child and adult is studied -- how it happens, when first it happens, how it can be nurtured, the relationship its maturity has, or not, to physical capacity. Writing and reading about experience is the way the western world tries to get a grip on essence, knowing all the while that it is the very act of doing something that sometimes releases one kind of intuitive grip. It can make a cold, hard, sharp-edged reality of pungently tactile material; it can turn a dream onto the copy machine.

With that said, we two have made some distillations out of our teaching that point to process in learning the artful quality of theological reflection. They are not unexpected: take experience, look at it, reflect upon the faith realities there exposed, conclude with general insights.

Chapter 10
General Theories

THE EXPERIENCE

In contemporary emphases on narrative theology there is acceptance of the truth that revelation is received through particularities. This does not make of Christianity less a revealed religion, but it sets the moments of truth into the context of lives, lives which are themselves God's truths. But surely the builders of the canon knew this, too. They had to select out of all the documents extant those that gave a broad but diverse tradition, trying to avoid the pitfalls either of no definition or of too stringent enclosure. This is always the church's problem; every church, even those declaring the most freedom from dogma, does either brush aside -- or sweep into its collation -- the matters important to it.

From a historical perspective, we speak of a mainstream of faith, of mainstream Christianity. Brought to us through the institution, this stream has had the effect of an onrushing momentum towards fuller flow and content. Looked at more pessimistically, the stream can seem to have been fuller at the beginning, now petering out into thinner brooklets as it loses the force of earlier "original" times. Let us, though, turn that imagery around a notch: can we regard the river as ever-flowing, fed by the tributaries of individual and ethnic stories, so that the accumulated force has within it a truth like the Gulf Stream but the river is neither just the accumulated water nor only the particularities of each contributing rivulet?

A sensation of teetering, as this implies, between encompassment and singularity may be a right attitude before God. Tentative yet firmly planted, we rock on the verge of discovery -- balance our lives against the edges of mystery. From this position, certain qualities of attitude are called for. They are related, indeed inversions of one overriding mood: humility. Reverence, care, regard, enjoyment, thanks as basic greetings "entre nous" are all included in the humble acceptance of the other person's self and tradition. If our experience in the stream of belief is to be offered as part of the valid revelation, then so is the experience of every other teller of encounter. The humble heart is the one who receives all this.

The word "humility" comes from the Latin word "humus," meaning fertile ground. Humility is the situation of the earth -- always there, taken for granted, trodden on, basic. Human earthiness admits of connections with creation and balks at special preference. Humanity.....humility.....underlies all our specialities. In faith we accept each other and our experiences first of all as fundamentally worthy; yet in faith we also say that they are especially distinctive and contributive. We humbly accept them.

Maria Harris brings together these ideas in a course (and now a book) entitled TEACHING AND RELIGIOUS IMAGINATION.[1] She speaks of the "thou" (from Buber) in the student, the holy being whom we teach. The imagery of her own teaching is that the ground between us -- learner and teacher or, more truthfully, learner and learner -- is holy space in which we are given the great gift of learning from each other and our Creator. We can learn from it in the art of theological reflection.

> It is not enough for (the teacher) to imagine the (person's) individuality, nor to experience him directly as a spiritual person and then to acknowledge him. Only when he catches himself "from over there," and feels how it affects one, how it affects this other human being, does he recognize the real limit, baptize his self-will in Reality and make it true will, and renew his paradoxical legitimacy.[2]

Buber says there is in education a "lofty asceticism;" it is there also in theological reflection where we become "humus" in God's hands.

LOOKING AT THE EXPERIENCE: ANALYSIS
For each person, life is restricted. By nature, all life is limited, for it sees from a perspective, not all perspectives. Health, age, education, imagination, family responsibilities, location are restrictive. Our perceptions of one another are limited, as are our energies and abilities. There will never be enough time, space, resources, or credibility...individually.

But these characteristics lose some of their limitations in community. My aging body's waning strength is complemented by my son's vigor. My more classical education supplements that of the craftsperson next door, and his experience teaches me skills. My location will draw narrower while my daughter's world-wide travel brings me in touch. My church's selective location in a fishing village is widened by the church's mission education.

To move beyond the boundaries which limit our perceptions, we try to be objective. Though new awareness can happen serendipitously, life cannot always wait until an encounter occurs. So we peel back the layers of restrictions which obscure our vision and examine the context, bias, interactions, and emotions of the situation.

In most of this, we rejoice. True, there is pain in some discovery of ways our shortsightedness has hurt us and others, but more often each partial view has lifted out an important detail. To return to the river imagery, each tributary adds depth to the river's main flow. Feminist and other minority claims have said this about their perspectives which have for so long been lost or denied by the mainstream male interpretation. The woman's voice has asked not only for place for her own experience; as a paradigm of neglect, she reminds us of other voices coming along in other tributaries -- voices of children, of the pained and shut-away, of the aging and weakening, of the artist and explorer, of the inarticulate. Indeed, we appreciate anew that voicing is only one means of expression along with painting, playing, dreaming, singing, pantomime - being, by itself.

FAITH REALITIES TO BE SEEN

Some years ago the late William Temple, Archbishop of Canterbury, shocked a gathering of church leaders by stating, "It is a mistake to think that God is concerned solely or even primarily with religion."[3] It has always been a temptation of the church to believe that the concerns of God are limited to its concerns.

Similarly, it has been the temptation of the university to believe that the concerns of education are primarily its concerns. Both institutions, because they **are** institutions, have looked with deep suspicion upon departures from their orthodoxies. Witness the attitude of the church to the Quakers or in recent years to modern art's attempts at religious understanding, or the professional educator's attitude toward the University of Chicago's education-at-home or educational TV. Both institutions resent departure from the status quo.

This kind of thinking which so easily divides life into compartments is not reality. Life is not yes or no; people are not ignorant or educated, profane or religious, secular or holy. Life is filled with combinations. And from each of them there erupts meaning. In theological reflection we look for God, with Dietrich Bonhoeffer, not in what we have **not** known or in what is special to the church but in what we **have** known in our experience.

INSIGHTS

More properly, this might be called conclusions, because we mean to ask the question, "what now?" Like the rattling of hailstones on a roof of corrugated iron, we may have heard the insistent reminders of experience and its pointers to faith, but what next will we do? Neither theological reflection nor spiritual formation can coerce answers. In the dialogue of reflection (between two persons, between God and person), mission will emerge. We expect it to come.

> A quite possibly apocryphal story about the philosopher, John Dewey, has him walking with his little boy on a wet, cold, windy day. The child, without rubbers, was splashing around in a puddle and a friend said, "You'd better get that boy out of the water. He'll get pneumonia."
> "I know it," the philosopher replied, "but I'm trying to find a way to make him want to get out of the water."

We are trying to find ways to want to act after thought, to be impelled by insights too deep to ignore, too important to deny.

Chapter 11
Some Theorists

In our shared and then diverging histories, Catholics and Protestants can both look to the practices of desert persons, the gathered communities (house churches), the retreat houses and sanctuaries for refreshment of dry souls, and the liturgies and adornments of buildings that memorialized and beckoned the faithful. Since then, since the sixteenth century, the two traditions have had different modes of spirituality, modes we frankly admit are far richer than our summary suggests. During the recent past, we have begun to notice each other again -- using both a common language and reappropriated disciplines.

The outlines of each strand still show. In brief, it can be seen in the work that we two brought together for resources in this chapter. The Catholic supplied four groups of theoreticians who have defined and outlined theological reflection or the way to spirituality. The Protestant referred to a myriad of writers who have supplied ideas and meditative "germs" for the devotional hour. Rich in thought and thing, the Catholic seeks to discipline the abundance and to hand on the discipline, whereas the Protestant regards the meditative time as essentially emptying and looks to the centering word for the way it will thrust revelation into the void. That is, the Catholic is filled, for spiritual growth, with the wealth of beauty in setting, liturgy, and prose. Protestant tradition has, on the other hand, emphasized the quiet time of getting away -- with perhaps a meditative guide and certainly a Bible -- to wait for leading or, more doctrinely, for revelation.

Simply to refer to our notes for this section indicates some of the difference in the Catholic and Protestant approaches, (though we readily admit that our notes may indicate far more the idiosyncratic nature of the authors). What we see in our notes is that the works of the Catholic theorists on whom we lean are blocked out and precise; they attempt comparison and contrast; they employ diagrams in columns, triads, or circles. The scribblings that refer to Protestant theorists cover dozens of references, give sentence quotations, suggest points of view. You may find these styles significant.

In Catholic theory the prime theorists for us are the Whiteheads who themselves acknowledge their dependence on Bernard Lonergan's process for noticing experience.[1] Experience in this case implies the experience of all time, collected experience. In his "heroic style", as Whiteheads call it, there is a system moving from research in all its historic forms to communication which is the relational end of the scheme.

James and Evelyn Whitehead develop a typology which shows both a plan and a set of attitudes. In their book, METHOD IN MINISTRY,[2] they graph the three poles of experience, tradition, and culture. Thus.....

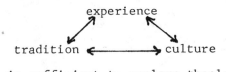

No one pole is sufficient to explore theology and life; they are interactive and interdependent. Additionally, they require a set of modes which describe the exploration. The method calls for

    1.) attending (seeking out the information),
    2.) assertion (engaging the information)
               and
    3.) decision (moving to pastoral action)

Elsewhere in this book we have applied the Whiteheads' model.

Robert Kinast[3] wants, with Lonergan and the Whiteheads, to start with experience and finish with implementation, but he treats tradition and culture differently. His middle steps are

                    contrast
    through extensification (in social sciences) and
    through intensification (in faith)

                    symbolization
    in narrative and poetry and
    in the objects and acts of devotion.

Taking justice as a key concern and with a full chapter on "the development debate," Joe Holland and Peter Henriot[4] develop a "pastoral circle" whose critical entry point is

> insertion (the "lively contact with the
>   experienced reality"),
> then social analysis ("the richness of
>   all their interrelationships"),
> theological reflection, and
> pastoral planning.

It would be much too simplistic to say that Catholics and Protestants can be compared as systematic and unsystematic, respectively; that characterization may, as we have suggested, describe us, the authors. But there is something to say about the ways in which we two arrive at our centrally important modes. Both of our traditions have received vast material throughout our histories -- much of it, we must always remember, a shared history. How do we move through this received plethora of wealth? One suggestion is to say that the Catholic takes in everything, stores it, and tries to be faithful by developing a system within which it may be scrutinized and employed ..... whereas the Protestant figuratively pushes away the incoming material and tries to become clear of "influence", taking up one proffered help at a time in a spirit of inquiry. It's as if the Catholic senses mystery in overwhelming beauty while the Protestant is only learning to trust such excess.

The prevailing attitude in Protestant meditation is listening for the yet-to-be-heard. Protestants take their Bibles, tracts, or devotional guides into the spareness of a room and in quiet, wearing faith in James Fowler's words as a "coat against (the) nakedness"[5] of mystery, wait for a new word from God. The mode is meditation and the expectation is revelation. Often, the action is testimony to God's presence or to God's single word of mission.

The incentive for this impulse towards emptying derives from the desperation or disquietude given all persons in the world. Believing that the world with its satisfactions and lures is ever stimulating the human being to satiety and often to poor (perhaps even evil) choice, the Protestant wants to retreat to a closet where direction will be given. Yet, with Douglas Steere, there is little asceticism in this retreat; ".....for desperate men there is always hope. It is the contented for whom all hope wanes."[6] The closet represents a place for regirding, for receiving that revealing word that sends back to the workplace the desperate-person-now-assured.

Letty Russell[7]"explores the impossible-possibil-
ity that God's partnership with us might set us free to
be partners with others" and that this shared enterprise
looks with hopes and dreams towards "God's tomorrow."
In Dorothee Soelle[8] is echoed this sense of the "not yet"
as the given in the new hope of the liberationist.

Edward Robinson[9] looks at children's experience
as recorded by older persons looking backward and finds
persuasive evidence for an early experience of overwhelming beauty and symmetry which is often understood
at the time as "sent" from outside. To the critique
that such insubstantial material does not stand well in
a scientific era, he quotes persons in scientific disciplines who are first of all "struck" by the precision
and beautiful orderliness of their material. Poincare,
writing on the creative process in mathematical thought,
speaks of

> 'a special aesthetic sensibility' as
> indispensable for real creative
> achievement and of the need for 'the
> feeling of mathematical beauty, of the
> harmony of numbers and forms.'[10]

Largely through the discipline of theological
reflection and the even more recent impetus towards disciplined spiritual formation, Protestants have looked
with Catholics (and to Catholics) for the processes
which can encourage development. Both have drawn on
their own traditions for inspiration - the Catholic to
the communities of faith who refined and defined the
spiritual life in ascetical and devotional living, and
the Protestant to the individuals who testified to personal experience in the "upper rooms" of their spiritual
struggles.

God moves in mysterious ways. Sometimes God
wins; sometimes, it must be admitted, God loses. Martin
Niemoeller was let out of prison. Dietrich Bonhoeffer
was not. An event may be evil in itself, yet still the
part of courage is to wrest from loss what profit we
can, to learn from error whatever lesson it may teach.
So acting, we do not glaze the fact nor turn bad into
good but we do, to the measure of the strength within
us, overcome evil. And that, we hold, is to act in the
way of God in this world.

Every Christian must not only rely on divine intervention, but on divine intention. This includes the development of persons who go through the day and the dark with invisible means of support, with no expectation that a celestial messenger will open all doors, smoothe all roads, or provide all answers. Sometimes we need to ask the hard questions as to whether we really want to open doors or clear our consciences. Camus said,

> Your business is not to clear your con-
> science but to learn to live with the
> burdens on your conscience.

In religion, we are not asked to make up our minds; we are asked to make up our lives. We may refuse to make up our minds, but our lives get made up in one way or the other. This intentionality is the route of theological reflection.

The Settings for Reflection

Early in this book, we have talked of occasions for theological reflection. You may well ask the difference between that topic and this one -- the places for reflection.

We have taken "occasions" (Chapter 3) to be those spontaneous times when we, without labeling, have been in fact reflecting theologically. The occasions, it is true, may be thoroughly structured, yet the reason for planning them had another programmatic objective into which, it was our intent to remind our reader, theological reflection is heard as a gracenote to a tune. No one would suggest that, once having studied theology, our professional reflection takes place only inadvertantly. We all identify times when thinking is coerced -- as in sermon or classroom planning. But the thrust of this book has been to say that reflection, though it is thought, takes another direction and mode; indeed, it is a disciplined excursion which can be taken inside the other preparations.

Hence, we take you into four such settings: classroom teaching, tutorial teaching, private study, and parish life.

Chapter 12
Places: Academy, Parish, Journal

IN ACADEMIA
    Teaching theological reflection is not easy,
because the very material defies "presentation." Like
the substance of faith, itself, one can talk about it,
but the point is to accept, appreciate, and practice.
What every good teacher knows is that the classroom must
become a place where hearing is allied to thinking,
speaking, and projecting (planning). To be most avoided
is the stance of one teacher described by Huston Smith,
"(He was) so nondirective on principle that students
used to say he not only didn't believe anything, he
didn't even suspect anything."

    Teachers have believed deeply that we should
capture the essence of our subject and order it so well
that it is easily appropriated. Led by this motive to
organize, refine, and present beautifully, we have also
realized that

> deeper and more fundamental than sexual-
> ity, deeper than the craving for social
> power, deeper even than the desire for
> possession, there is a still more gener-
> alized and more universal craving in the
> human make-up. It is the craving for
> knowledge of the right direction - for
> orientation.[1]

That is what we seek: orientation for the faithful. And
our word to you, the reader, is that the classroom somehow be the arena for theological reflection and not
alone for hearing about it.

    Classroom work can take such forms as the fol-
lowing:

> - take one or all of the typologies des-
>   cribed and apply them to case studies.
> - write case studies, each from the
>   point of view of a particular theolog-
>   ical position.
> - trace out the myriad possibilities of
>   action when culture, tradition, and
>   experience interpose varying configu-

ations on the same doctrinal point.
- give testimony in the form of personal
  stories.
- plan ways of bringing to a congregation some of this learning.
- work with each other in pairs, encouraging insight in one another.

Your expertise as teacher will suggest to you, with
these hints, any number of exercises that will encapsu-
late the flavor of theological reflection.

CASE in which a TEACHER of THEOLOGICAL RE-FLECTION MADE HIMSELF VULNERABLE before the CLASS[2]

Goal for this class period:
> to apply theological reflection to our own
> stories.

Method:
> the teacher's own journey experience in-
> side this classroom (a temporary confer-
> ence, away from his own teaching post)

Analysis of the present:
> Some students are feeling that their ex-
> pectations have not been met.
> Some matters that have surfaced have not
> been resolved - or even processed.
> I, the teacher, am experienced as distant,
> giving content but not myself.
> Some persons have, though, acknowledged
> learning a methodology, and that consti-
> tutes a sufficient learning experience for
> them.

My own experience of the class:
> An intense and honest group
> Persons who are painfully vulnerable in
> their place of ministry
> Ones who are in need of relating their
> ministerial call to this wounding they
> have experienced
> Persons willing to share their open wounds

My culture shock:
> I feel trapped without car and city envi-
> rons.
> The usual period for my retreats has been
> four days, not six weeks. It feels like
> too-prolonged cessation.
> An only child, I have left my invalid
> mother at home; I feel guilty for depriv-

ing her not only of physical presence but
of emotional support.
My usual ministry is in an all-male environment. Here I am with a largely female
group. It is unsure.

My response:
I have thrown up a shield to protect myself from the tide of passion I feel in
this place. I don't want to be consumed by
the feelings I know could erupt. But now
they have, in a sense, erupted anyway. By
trying to keep myself safe in an unsure
setting, I have provoked the very response
I feared.
There are similarities between this and
another time when I was told outright that
I could only be a good pastor if I were to
share more of my humanity; I am remembering that many capacities in me collide:
- my penchant for solitariness and my
  priestly vows
- my competitive spirit
- my desire for acceptance and excellence.
     (These sound like pride!)

My Learning:
I have reopened the findings of an earlier
time, and that speaks strongly to me of
their truth. In spiritual direction and
prayerful reflection, I will review the
baggage I take to every place and try a-
gain to model the grace which I teach.

We present this case to demonstrate the use of theological reflection typologies in relation to the very classroom, itself. It has a strength of personal involvement,
but it takes the risk of coming close to clinical scrutiny. You will judge whether it is appropriate, but remind yourself that that there is the hard-to-determine
division between
        personal experience/vulnerability/ modeling
                            and
        master teacher/priest/pastor.

IN THE PARISH
     Dialogue and collaboration between pastor and
parishioner can take the form of theological reflection.
Take only one point, Jesus' frequent reference to the

Kingdom of God; Jesus spoke of it more often than he spoke of anything else. At times he spoke as though it had already come (present reality).

> The time is fulfilled and the Kingdom of
> God is at hand.

At other times he spoke as though it had not yet come (future hope).

> Thy Kingdom come.....You are to watch
> for it; it will come like a thief.

This apparent contradiction has puzzled people. Some have explained it away, but there is another way to hear it. Anybody who has had a garden knows of both reality and hope.

> A person has a garden
> One plows, plants, cultivates
> It is a present fact.

Yet a person always speaks of a garden in terms of the future. One plans to rearrange it, to start other kinds of seeds, to improve varieties; it is a garden now but only a hint of the garden to come. The Kingdom, as our garden, is both present fact and future hope.

In each parish, theological reflection can be the process that cultivates, plants, weeds, and waters. It is a nurturing place. In this imagery lie all the organizational ideas of parish life (commitment, teaching, pastoral outreach and sustenance, vision, and mission). Through all is the discernment of the future and our place in it now.

IN A JOURNAL
In classroom and parish, nearly everyone is familiar with the discipline of keeping a journal. Even library and course reading lists have rediscovered the journals of our ancestors, and especially through the feminist movement they have helped us to capture the tone of discipline and flair and life-penetration heretofore lost in the annals of revised history.

Journals allow theological reflection that is so close to Being, itself, any other writing form would not be private enough. In a way, they are attempts to take an objective view of a subjective reality. Privacy is a key note; published journals are almost misnomers unless the writer is able to maintain the seclusion needed to separate him/herself from the inquiries that follow self-revelation. Yet journal writing does plumb the depths of self, thereby exposing subterranean streams that are common to others. There is sometimes the discovery of a collective unconscious and when this happens, there is reason to publish and share the commonalities.

Caution suggests that the cast thrown over printed work is different from the aura of a private effort. As soon as journals are deemed ready for print, for public consumption, they tend towards a pre-established point of view; they often sound like tracts.

Diaries of travels or of more discerning experiences like workcamps or worker-priest assignments are known from the start to have the seed of "usefulness." They are useful.....and they can be theological reflection. But we do not call them journals.

The journal, safeguarded in a sanctuary and written in a rush of feeling or idea, is exactly the work of self-discovery. Used theologically, it is discovery of an orientation in faith. It is this precisely because it is not intended to be spread before anyone, though journal writers frequently take their jottings to someone they honor for sharing and enlightenment. This is our choice.

Chapter 13
Habits: Tutorial, Biography, Supervision

THE REGULAR TUTORIAL

In Oxford and Cambridge Universities, in the thirteenth century, the tutorial method was set by the common practice of students gathering in small groups around a master teacher. Often, this work was even more face-to-face, an arrangement between the teacher and one or two students. In this tutorial (called supervision at Cambridge), the value is of two minds in sharing and confrontation--usually over an essay required of the student for each session. Good tutors are scholars and sharp analysts. They are alert to the best and weakest points in a student's work, and they advance learning by being in turn critical, tolerant, and encouraging.

Such a system throughout a university of many thousand students is expensive in energy and finances. In the church, its counterpart took place as apprenticeship; students in colonial New England, for instance, apprenticed themselves to church ministers who studied with them both biblical texts and learned commentaries as well as sharing the responsibilities of the daily round.

The tutorial has produced over these years a high quality of written thoughtful language. It is an intellectual exercise in content and form, and it can strengthen and toughen the minds of teacher and student. Group tutorials come nearer to the idea of seminars, but they keep emphasis on a group not exceeding five or so persons who aim at rigor of content and presentation. They can give shape and vitality to theological reflection.

The following excerpt is from George Bailey's reflection on C.S. Lewis in the tutorial session:[1]

> The Oxford and Cambridge tutorial system is based, as it were, on the direct confrontation of tutor and undergraduate. The form of the system is simple: one essay a week on a set topic...... Ordinarily the reading of the essay takes up the first fifteen minutes of the hour. In the remaining time, the tutor attacks

the essay's argument or lack of one and the undergraduate does his best to defend his work...... As far as I know, no undergraduate ever dared appear for a tutorial with Lewis with his essay only half finished.

Lewis had three standard forms of comment on an essay.
If the essay was good: "There is a good deal in what you say."
If the essay was middling: "There is something in what you say."
If the essay was bad: There may be something in what you say."

His other fairly standard comments were: "too much straw and not enough bricks",
and
"not with brogans, please; slippers are in order when you proceed to make a literary point."
Lewis was sparing in his compliments. The highest I know of was:
"Much of that was very well said,"
but he was quick to notice any excellence of usage. He spent five minutes praising one word I used to describe Dryden's poetry (the word was "bracing").

If the three years at Oxbridge with weekly hour-long tutorials is the basis for a superb education, then weekly sessions for theological reflection may be occasions full of promise. Writing in advance and taking seriously the fact and reflection, the dimension of education may be immeasurable.

The tutorial style of teaching engages students in a special style of conversation. Martin Buber, whose pervasive theme is dialogue, says that in teaching there is a "lofty asceticism":

an asceticism which rejoices in the world, for the sake of the responsibility for a realm of life which is entrusted to us for our influence but not our interference.....[2]

In this dialogue, when the teacher practices the experience of being in the place of the student, the living place, the teacher knows two things:

> that (he) is limited by otherness, and
> .....that (he) receives grace by being
> bound to the other. [3]

In the meeting between these two, the threshold of an invisible door is crossed where inner isolation between persons ends. Developments are unpredictable. Two centers gravitate towards each other, so that by standing at the same point each comes to see what the other sees. Along with the movement of the two centers, there occurs a coalescence of horizons and ceilings. In speech a common pact is both discovered and created.

In theological reflection, the mutual stimulation may enhance the learning of facilitator as well as student.

> In one of our classes, a student said,
> "The more we realize how profound the
> issues are, the more we realize how
> shallow our understanding really is. I
> believe that sets up a tension which
> becomes the catalyst for theological
> reflection. When one has a shallow un-
> derstanding of something profound, there
> is a hunger created." [4]

In satisfying the hunger, both intellect and emotion may be stirred, but the purpose is not to avoid difficulty. It is to produce character and strength adequate to meet life's burdens.

Helmut Thielicke has a chapter in his book, A LITTLE EXERCISE for YOUNG THEOLOGIANS,[5] in which he observes that the person who studies theology must watch carefully to see whether the thinking is done in the third person rather than in the second person. We might remember, he points out, that Anselm begins his argument for deity in his PROLOGUE with a prayer, and that his dogmatics were therefore prayed dogmatics.

THE USE OF BIOGRAPHY

Biography elicits response. Inherently, we are comparers of experience, running reported accounts through the sieve of our own memories. Immediately, we say,

"That sounds familiar" or "I can imagine that"
or we say,
"That is outside possibility for me, but it
interests me" or
"I can't connect with that and don't want to
try."

For this reason, biography is a way into the
center of subject matter that appears distant. Knowledge or belief that is acted out on the stage of life
asks the viewer to handle that material. And so, we have
found it to be a means -- a variously alive means -- of
bringing to theological reflection an engaging quality.
From parish to classroom, it has brought into conversation the details and behaviors of important persons'
lives with a pressure that calls out enrichment, calls
for contesting with "why's", and sometimes calls up
adaptation.

In a suburban parish, each week we met
for worship and discussion on the life
and thought of Dietrich Bonhoeffer,
Pierre Teilhard de Chardin, Reinhold
Niebuhr, Mark Twain, Dorothy Day, Carl
Jung, C.S. Lewis, Paul Tillich, Dorothee
Soelle, Albert Schweitzer, Martin Luther
King, and others. Opening worship took
as theme a portion of that person's writings, then prayer and silent reflection.

Over coffee, discussion worked to increase theological literacy and to bring
new thought to contemporary issues and
the church's teachings. Ethical responsibility, specifically as Christians,
was the principle reason for being together.

Since then, I have taken the method into
the classroom.[6] It cannot replace systematic study but alongside more formal
presentations, biography integrates
lifetime's struggles. It is clear that
the events of these peoples' lives deeply influenced their systematic thinking
and the tone and content of their ministries. Bonheoffer's work on ETHICS cannot be fully understood without the
knowledge of his return to Nazi Germany

-- his ethical response to faith -- his involvement in the resistence, his imprisonment, and his death. LETTERS AND PAPERS FROM PRISON[7] gives background for the ethics.

But this is, you could say, still distancing from the lifetimes of those, like our parishioners or students, who have not been "on the edge" of ethnic or cultural oppression. Our own vignettes are not so grand or generic. Ah, but here we have come to appreciate autobiography set next to biography. Every life does have meaning and it is a truism to say that if it is of importance to no one else, it certainly is to the subject. So after we study biographies of famed people, we begin to look at our own lives -- autobiography.

Within the circle of friendship for each of us, there are a few persons who are special to us. Perhaps they encouraged us in the right moment. Their biographies entered into our autobiography. It may even be that they did not know they were examples for us; but in some situation, having suffered a kind of failure, they yet lived their lives with no apparent bitterness, just calm and steady performance of whatever work their strength would allow. Generally, we find they had a center of interest outside of self. In them, biography and theology formed a harmony in life which sang a redemptive melody for us.

Biography and autobiography both show theology in the living. Autobiography can be poignantly or embarrassingly revealing or self-serving. For most of us, others have a better perspective on our life than we do; we notice that perspective by reading biography or by hearing commentary on our spoken autobiography as we offer it in a small group. Biographers see a highlight or trend that frequently is hidden from the subject of the biography. Both autobiography and biography have significant but different roles in theological reflection.

It has been suggested that the greatness of a life can be measured by the greatness of a moment. But the great moments often are not recognized by us as great until later -- much later. Hence, the realm of autobiography; it is a retrospective done by ourselves. Who can identify in the past that precise moment when life began to come together, to make sense for us? Who knows the day when the God who is always coming was

99

first received? Few. We see it as we take up our auto-
biographies. Significance stands out because we look for
it, as steppingstones in our development (Ira Progoff's
term).

Biography helps to put life into ecological balance. God's dealings with us are infinitely gentle, sim-
ple, and subtle. We have a place in God's sovereignty --
in God's ecological balance -- but to know the place
requires the eyes of faith, often the eyes of another in
faith. Since the factors in this ecological balance are
living factors, so must be our response. Thus, reflection as a continuing catalyst in the private life and
community worship life of the Christian is crucial. A.
N. Whitehead speaks of the movement from God-the-abyss
to God-the- enemy to God-the-friend. Tracing the path of
faith in our lives, we may see a similar trail.

Perhaps life for us is more like a forest on
Cape Cod. If we stroll through such a forest, we will be
struck by the large number of fallen trees. A forest is
a cemetary of once-living forms that soon rot and return
to the earth whence they came. A forest is also living
trees from whose arrow-like trunks in the spring shoots
new life, straight to the sunlight overhead. A forest is
fresh every year; every leaf, every pine needle is a
chlorophyll factory, fueling the engine of new life. But
most of all, a forest is a robust, growing, mighty
surge of new life, creating new forms, enlarging old
forms. The dead forms make a rich loam, nourishing living forms at whose roots they lie.

A life is not unlike a forest. It has its living
forms, its discarded past, its growing margins, and its
pulsing interior life. So it is with life and theological reflection. Biography, and indeed autobiography, may
give the perspective to serve the unlimited will of God
in the organic forest of life.

Howard Thurman once said that the simplest definition of art is the activity by which people realize
the place of their ideals in their lives. We are all
artists in this sense.

Let us take an extended example. The use of biography in establishing a habit of theological reflection
comes clearer, for instance, in the events of Martin
Luther King's life. The inexorable tide of particular
details moves him from the experience of raw prejudice,
to the struggle as a parson's son with faith, and then

100

to his giving himself as a theological and pastoral con-
signment to justice.

In STRIDE TOWARD FREEDOM[8] (THE MONTGOMERY STORY)
Dr. King describes the early years in Atlanta
when he watched the Ku Klux Klan on its nightly
rides and saw the courtroom's tragic injustice.
In spite of the wishes of his father who never
wanted either Martin or his brother to work
around white people because they were known for
unjust behavior, Martin, in his teens, took a
job in a plant where both blacks and whites
were hired. Here he saw firsthand economic injustice, exploitation that was meted out to
both whites and blacks because they were without status. At Morehouse College, he read Thor-
eau's ESSAY on CIVIL DISOBEDIENCE and met for
the first time outside the Scriptures, the theory of non-violent resistence.

By 1948 at Crozer Theological Seminary, King
was ready for the thought of Walter Rauschen-
busch who provided a theological base for his
social concern. Now he began to see that social, political, and economic matters are as
much a part of faith as personal salvation. The
individualism of his upbringing was challenged;
especially for his own community -- black people in the south -- playing together was the
only way their symphony of justice had a chance
of being either played or heard. He soon learned criticism even of Rauschenbush whose optimism and assumptions about inevitable progress
were too certain for King.

Many have wondered at King's "dabbling" with
unpopular ideas like communism. But, ever the
scholar, he read the original documents, DAS
KAPITAL and the MANIFESTO, and rejected their
materialistic interpretation of history.

> This I could never accept, for as a
> Christian I believe that there is a cre-
> ative, personal power in this universe
> who is the ground and essence of all
> reality -- a power that cannot be ex-
> plained in materialistic terms.[9]

Though differing with communism's ethical rela-
tivism and political totalitarianism, King

101

heard Marx's strong protest for he had experienced the gulf between superfluous wealth and abject poverty.

It was Mahatma Gandhi's work that put together for King the ethic of love with social responsibility. Almost an incidental hearing, Martin had traveled to Philadelphia to hear Dr. Mordecai Johnson, President of Howard University, preach on his trip to India. Through Johnson, King met Gandhi; he loaded up with books and discovered that a different interpretation of Jesus' ethics could enlarge the scope from individual to social relationships. Until then, King had read the teachings of Jesus on forgiveness, going the second mile, and turning the other cheek as effective person-to-person mission, but he expected that another ethic was needed in group and national dynamics. In Gandhi, however, he saw the love ethic made into an efficient and forceful political strategy. This philosophy of nonviolent resistence became the cornerstone of Dr. King's theology and ethics.

Corrections were to come, of course. The work of Reinhold Niebuhr, specifically, provided a healthy seasoning of realism to his social ethics. Niebuhr helped King to see the difference between non-resistance to evil and nonviolent resistence to evil.

> Gandhi resisted evil with as much vigor and power as the violent resisters, but he resisted with love instead of hate.[10]

Niebuhr's realism and insight into human nature gave King courage. Further work for his Ph.D. degree at Boston University added the insights of personalism.

Out of the integration of theological with biographical insights came the famous "Letter from a Birmingham Jail.

> Injustice anywhere is a threat to justice everywhere. We are caught in an inescapable network of mutuality, tied in a single garment of destiny. What affects one directly, affects all indirectly.

In STRENGTH TO LOVE,[11] Dr. King has a sermon entitled "A Tough Mind and a Tender Heart," taken from Matthew 10:16: "Be ye therefore wise as serpents and innocent as doves." In this, King shows his capacity for rigorous dialectical thinking -- warm compassion with a stern sense of justice. One of the martyrs of our day, we are haunted by him.

> Whether we think of the arms race or our personal frustrations, the insight is that violence brings only temporary peace; violence, by creating many more social problems than it solves, never brings permanent peace.[12]

The life of Dr. King illustrates the joining of personal with communal history. Further, it shows the courage that must follow intellectual discovery if vision is to be realized. The problems of any day -- racism, sexism, the unequal distribution of wealth -- call for private imagery turned into public imagining with commitment to act.

One hopes that theological reflection can invite the integration of biography with theology. But mission is the end of theological reflection. For us, Jesus is the way. Everytime we stay overnight in a theological motel and find the system comfortable, we are called on to continue the journey.

Much depends on the mood of our study and journey. Dr. King understood the church as the perpetually penultimate realm where the reign of God is continually being presented to humanity. Life hands out negative replies and we are tempted to make final judgments when we are disappointed. But this is the battleground on which the tension between the divine and history, the transcendent and immanent, intersect. God's reign is at hand and, at the same time, yet to be realized.

Our faith tells us that each person is valuable. Paul made this clear in his description to the Romans of our membership in one body; it is value within diversity. Stereo recordings called "Music Minus One" give amateur musicians a chance to enter the realm of the professional orchestra by playing the part that has been left out. There is no "music" without that part. In symphonies, one musician takes the lead from time to time, but the music is never complete without every instru-

103

ment.

Each of us can do that. Through reflection on
the biographies of brothers and sisters, we can find our
part -- the one without which the symphony of life would
be unmusical. Others' biographies set beside our auto-
biographies are a testing ground on which we can envi-
sion a harmonious or discordant participation.

PERIODIC SUPERVISION
Seminaries have developed departments of field
education to provide professional oversight in the practical education of future pastors. In the field, the
apprenticeship model remains an honorable way to learn
ministerial content and skills; besides this technique
which is much like "shadowing", there are team models,
associate models, and agency settings in which craft and
expertise are predominant. In all, supervision is given
by a person who engages all aspects of the work
assignments, theory, and theology.

A pastoral supervisor is an educator in
partnership with the seminary. Having the mind of
co-learner, the supervisor acts as pedagogue -- teaching
the art of ministry and drawing out the student's own
skills and creativity. Taking pedagogy in its meaning
"to accompany the learner to school," the supervisor is
both leader and companion.

Essential in the supervisory process is
theological reflection. At the Toronto School of
Theology, for instance, there was established a task
force who concluded the following:

> We on the Task Force believe that the
> key part of theological education should
> be training students to do theological
> reflection on their experience.....Theo-
> logical reflection serves an integrative
> role in two senses.
> 1.) it strives to integrate our experi-
> ence, theological tradition, various
> disciplines of knowledge and faith;
> 2.) it strives to integrate the person
> himself/herself (spiritual formation).
> The purpose of theological reflection is
> to help us become more integrated indiv-
> iduals, more in touch with God, our-
> selves, and our world.[3]

As mentor in the art of theological reflection, the supervisor brings to work all the discipline thus far described in this book. Because the supervisor is responsible for introduction into all of ministry, the art of reflection is an intentional style penetrating everything. The learner is held accountable not only for the performance of a task but also for articulating theological connections. He or she is held to this task by several inbuilt requirements. In the Boston Theological Institute most students 1.) submit weekly written reports describing an event in ministry and giving some theological overview and 2.) work with lay committees who make a covenant with the school to share the student's local experience. Much like the tutorial discipline, these measures insure regularity and an expected piece of written work. The growth is intended towards an integrated pastoral identity.

> One pastoral supervisor submitted the following: I would begin from the theological understanding of "call." We are called by God to serve Jesus Christ, our Lord and Saviour, and one dimension of our service is to minister God's love to our neighbor. The concept of the priesthood of all believers is the theological affirmation that every believer should be involved in Christian ministry. One part of my role as supervisor is to help the student to grasp this dimension, beginning with examination of personal salvation history. It continues with general Christian activity and its motivation. A strong emphasis is on caring and the biblical imperative "to love one another."
>
> There is in my tradition a second use of the word "call", specifically call to the ministry. God, by the Spirit and through the Church, prepares and calls some persons to full time professional leadership. A majority of these are called to parish ministry. Thus, a second concern for me is to help the student to sense and accept the call. It is important to be able to affirm God's activity in the choice of vocation, to be able to identify and develop one's gifts, and to identify persons of

significance in one's journey. The
motivation for ministry and the emphasis
on caring are transferable.

Another supervisor describes supervision in
this way:
The call to ministry is a call to leadership
and a vocation in the Church ("church" broadly
understood as wherever Christians are at work).
Within the setting of the parish, I feel this
is best expressed in the concept of
"pastoring." My central task in field education
is to share what it is to pastor a
congregation; I want to show how to do it and
involve the student so it can be examined. It
is important that the learner is exposed to all
spiritual and temporal dimensions of the role
-- worship, liturgy, prayer, and preaching; the
sacraments, rites of the church, and pastoral
visitation.

These are the things students readily associate
with ministry. What they sometimes are not so ready to
acknowledge as their responsibility is the temporal
dimension of hard work, long hours, and executive
leadership.

The second major theological concern of my
supervision is the mission of the church. I
understand the Great Commission to be the
marching orders of the Church -- namely, to
lead others to Jesus Christ. This is the rubric
under which I regard my work with a supervisee.
Implicit in the Commission is to prepare others
to lead towards Jesus. Thus, wherever there is
the opportunity for a church to be involved in
the field education of seminarians, I think it
is the church's mission to do it. At this
point, supervision is very incarnational --
giving embodiment to the words of Jesus and his
life's message. Thus, the motivation for
supervision is Christ's own command and our
obedient involvement in enabling others to
minister in his name.[14]

Section III
Peering in the Window:
Two reflectors in Dialogue

Chapter 14
Peace and Justice

DAN:
The Christian gospel speaks directly to that isolated person who dwells within the heart of everyone of us. Its message is this: although solitude may be the last word so far as we are concerned, it is not the last word so far as God is concerned. We know the first and last moments of life are spent inside our own selves, and often we are told that the questions of faith are born in this essential loneliness which, for some more than others, feels unbearable. Between those times, when life is always in the midst of something -- some group, some crisis, some palpable environment -- we may try to shut ourselves off from others and from God, too. It is the relentlessness of the "Hound of Heaven" that is the truth we want to affirm for its sustenance and the truth we want to evade for its requirement. Wanting to be both chosen and forgotten, depending upon our condition, humans twist and turn between the reality of Christ's reconciling love and the agony of estrangement.

Humans hide from conscience today, as ever, and to know the Author of conscience is to know in one moment two faces of God: God's imperative and God's unconditional love. What agonies they are! They fulfill as they tug; they invite as they repel because they claim.

We hide from God because we prefer to deal with religious and moral matters not directly, but obliquely and casually. We hide from God lest we feel the aweful weight of choice and daring. But there is no place to hide. Life comes after us; today becomes tomorrow; tomorrow is now. This is the especial warrant for reflecting on issues -- in this case, the wide issue of justice and peace.

There are areas in life which are not obvious, which we do not stumble on and say, "It was here in the nature of things; I discovered it, entered into it, and grasped it." In marriage, in national life and education, as in almost all important aspects of living, the revelation comes first and the analysis and discovery follow it. These events overtake us first and then we try to understand them. It is as if another dimension of life were added and we came into relationship with it and could only say that beyond height and depth and breadth there lies another dimension which deserves to be taken as seriously as height and depth and breadth.

RON:
What you say about revelation's coming first and being followed by analysis and discovery is very true. I have never been a social activist, and I have rebelled against being called a "priest of the sixties." Yet my dedication is full, and my reasons are based in three experiences which were revelations: a class in pastoral theology, a summer course with Paulo Frieri, and the assassination of Archbishop Romero in El Salvadore.

In the class dealing with ministry in an urban setting, a seminarian said the following:
Our parents had to work for a living;
let the poor work for what they get.
My first response was instant anger at this student's insensitivity. But I am a teacher with emphasis in theological reflection. Reflection led me to understand that the student was representative of the children and grandchildren of middleclass American families who had grown up during the struggles of the depression. Having survived to move up the social ladder, they were in some senses justly proud of their accomplishment, and they felt diminished if others were able to come to a condition of "comfort" without similar effort. Their reflection lacked the pole of cultural consideration. Their perhaps excessive pride blinded them to cultural and systemic differences. I vowed then and there to do all I could to sensitize my students to the plight of the poor, a plight often rooted in social injustice.

It was not so much the educational methodology of Paulo Frieri that influenced me, but his personal witness as a Catholic Christian. When asked why he remained a Catholic in Brazil where so many members of the religious hierarchy appeared to be on the side of the non-poor, he responded that he loved his church and that its leaders were human. He said he saw a gradual transformation of these church leaders by the dedicated work of the missionaries who became one with the poor. I had to ask myself the question: where in my ministry was my work directly involved with the needy? I could no longer remain separated, so I began to work in prison ministry where raw life was spread before me. I had to show God's love in a seedbed of violence.

Archbishop Romero's last words exerted a transformative influence on me.

> We have just heard in the gospel that those who surrender to the service of people through love of Christ will live like the grain of wheat that dies. This hope comforts us as Christians. We know that every effort to improve society, above all when society is so full of injustice and sin, is an effort that God blesses, wants, and demands. We have the security of knowing that what we plant, if nourished with Christian hope, will never fail.
> This Holy Mass, this Holy Eucharist, is clearly an act of faith. This body broken and blood shed for human beings encourages us to give our body and blood up to suffering and pain as Christ did -- not for self, but to bring justice and peace to our people. Let us be intimately united in faith and hope at this moment.[1]

(Minutes after this, Archbishop Romero was shot to death.)

His witness and that of four church women who were murdered, also, made me realize that I could no longer distance myself from issues of peace and justice. I cannot take **every** opportunity (although that is the hope of every fresh commitment) because I am bound to my place and time. But I can take what opportunity lies in my path. I became part of a Task Force on Education for Peace, and I have agreed to teach an ecumenical course on the subject.

You are right: these events -- a class, a course, and a homily -- were for me revelations which upon analysis led to discovery and change.

DAN:
The poor of the inner city and the witness of both Paulo Freire and Archbishop Romero were transformative in your life. I would like to move us beyond the emotional impact which these events had on your life and explore the causes of the poverty and oppression of the inner city and Brazil and El Salvadore. Our society has

given us plenty of sociological and political reasons; we are surfeited with facts and even when they do not coalesce, there is sufficient material for mission. Where we do not give attention, either politically or theologically, is in the area of will and resolve. Why do we not get ourselves committed? These are the questions of the church, of theological reflection.

I believe, with you and a lot of others, that the rage felt by victims of our world society is the result of injustice coming from the first world. It is the power of those of us in countries of physical abundance that has kept depressed those people who live in the third and fourth worlds. I want to think theologically about that.

In the church we usually say that our ethical choices in places of oppression are practicing justice or love. Christians are drawn to the option of love, but Reinhold Niebuhr has correctly pointed out that to leap immediately to speaking of love is too quick and cheap. To us in the privileged world, justice may seem empty and unfilling compared to the warmth of love, but it is quite clear that third world persons would settle, at least in the present, for a large shipment of justice (in the form of food, shelter, and the means of crafting their own societies) before they would ask for the embodiments of love.

Even our own country has come to see that though manipulated effort toward justice is not enough, it is basic. Displaced and unemployed workers from the middle class (unimaginable, we used to think) whose lives still have in place for them the communities of concern and love are, nevertheless, justly indignant that the United States system "for all" has let them down and there seems to be not even a wedge back into it. Justice is the bed in which we can nurture love.

Love without justice is cheap. And justice without love leads to despair; it can be cold and calculating. Robert Louis Stevenson once said that we all sit down to a table of consequences. True. The interrelationship of justice with love and peace is the problem.

There is no place where religion becomes the enemy of faith and of the people more obviously than where the church becomes preoccupied with its own institutional stability and its own precise position as a center of power over against the rest of society.

When I was in school, I asked questions about humanity's mindless aggression and self-destructive behavior. I was told that the human being is no more than an animal among animals, a kind of ape with savage biology and killer instincts over whom society brings controlling and humanizing influences. This cynical and overly pessimistic view of humankind gained popularity as a rationalization for the absurdity of human behavior and a mandate for great organizational programs of enlightenment.

But the killing of one's own kind is almost unknown in the animal kingdom, except in courtship contests. The killers of the animal world are predators who only kill to eat. The great apes are shy, unaggressive, almost exclusively vegetarian, and live cooperatively in societies or groups of one hundred or less. Elephants do not eat lambs -- or other elephants.

The human animal is a species whose biologically inherited behavior can be modified by society, which is in turn a human creation. The great variety of different cultures created by humanity sets us apart from apes and other animal species. If humans were innately aggressive, all humanity would inevitably be aggressive in highly predictable standard behavior.

Some societies are aggressive and some are non-violent. Human aggression is expressed in widely varying ways -- ranging from debate, verbal insults and threats, to attempts at physical dominance in hand-to-hand combat or warfare. There is a great difference between human behavior and the reflexive and highly stereotypical aggressive responses made by lower animals. The human aggressive response is shaped not by instinct so much as by the particular culture in which the individual lives.

RON:
Your response raised three areas of concern for me:
- my focus on justice alone which you
  say can lead to despair
- the response of the church
- the possibility of a non-violent response

I have begun to see that justice flows from love and mercy. Justice without love is impossible. Cardinal Medeiros, the late Archbishop of Boston, gave on July 4, 1983 an address entitled "Stewards of This Heritage" in

111

which he stated

> It is from this truth of human dignity
> -- which is rooted in the fact that we
> are created in God's image -- that the
> meaning of the values of justice and
> active mutual love must be determined in
> our communities. Justice in public life
> is not simply the protection of self-
> interest or individual independence. It
> is a structured order of public life by
> which we realize our worth as persons
> together.[2]

I as pastor/teacher do not have a right to be uninvolved
with justice issues. If I believe in human dignity and
the commandment of love, I must begin to examine them as
motivations for action.

Your remarks concerning the church as an institution which can become self-centered and power-seeking
affirm my experience of Freire and his relationship to
the institutional church in Brazil. I, too, am a Roman
Catholic who loves his church. I have given my life in
service. I must, however, think of the human side of
this institution, the sinfulness in all people. As the
church offers me forgiveness when I sin, I too must be
ready to accept and forgive the institutional church
when it sins. In loyalty and love, I have a responsibility to offer a challenge to the church -- but also to
wait in patience for God's loving spirit to work.

I agree that humanity is not by nature violent
and aggressive. Yet we are surrounded by violence, and I
find it very difficult to read the newspapers, turn on
television, or even to listen to the radio. You could
easily conclude that, indeed, violence is constitutive
of humanity. Your reflection on the rational nature of
human beings, who are influenced by culture is challenging. If the Christian way of life is supposed to point
the way to the reign of God, then each one of us has to
work towards culture's transformation. The way of Mahatma Gandhi comes to mind. He was able to transform an oppressive society without the use of violent force. It is
strange that those who work in the name of love become
the martyrs -- beginning with Jesus to the modern day
witness of Gandhi, Martin Luther King, Jr., Archbishop
Romero, and nameless others. I have to ask myself
whether I am willing to give myself so totally -- even
unto death.

DAN:

We all have to ask a similar question. But, you see, from my perspective, it is not so strange that the deaths of these martyrs have taken place. They represent -- we see when we are analytical -- the expected outcome of a society's misplaced power and misunderstanding of the interrelationship of justice and love. Justice without love is cold and unsustaining; it would soon be forsaken as calculating and "inhumane." But it is inhumane not to be just. Love without justice is soft and without structure; it cannot deal with the complexities of life. But it is inhumane not to love all. A dialectic! Unresolvable unless we hold up both sides at once.

In this reflection on justice and peace we are confronted by challenges. We see both the evils in society and the good to which those you mention gave witness. Niebuhr's observation[3] that the possibilities of evil grow with the possibilities of good must be included in any serious theological reflection. Our century which has seen the horror of Hitler and the Holocaust now experiences a gnawing sense of impending nuclear doom. Do we have insight from theology concerning these issues?

The theology expressed by the churches can be confusing. As Gabriel Fackre[4] observes, the Religious Right often supports nuclear power. The Catholic Bishops have opposed the expansion of nuclear weapons, a stand applauded by mainline Protestant journals like "The Christian Century." All now express horror over the Holocaust.

Those who have known me know that I have been comfortable with the word "dialectic" and use it frequently. I lately experience that word differently and often use a different imagery; I like to consider myself now on the boundary-line. In reflecting on the reasons for this, I suspect that I am now more willing to live with apparent contradiction without looking for some rational synthesis. For Hegel, the very nature of reason was the thinking out of contradiction. The word "dialectic" in its original meaning was "the art of debate." More and more, I now believe that the resolution of the problem of human suffering and evil comes from commitment and action, not debate.

Also, it seems to me that the structure of Christian faith is symphonic rather than logical. There is logic implicit within its minor themes, but the overall movement of its affirmations presents a dissonant situation in which contraries are simultaneously acknowledged and disavowed, in which resolution and peace are somehow attained -- but not without the price of conflict, pain, and suffering, not without a sense of taking the conflict into oneself, of bearing the burden. In short, it is not without the cross.

I remember, as in parenthesis, a comment of Krister Stendahl's from a lecture on the idea of fulfillment and sacrifice in Christianity. His reminder was that we can define what the cross means for us, personally, but we can never define what the cross means for someone else. That is, it is easy for me to say that resolution comes with the price of pain and suffering if I am making a global statement of principle which works out, in fact, to mean the suffering of someone else. It is easy, but it is not right. My right to say that the cross is required comes only with my assessment of my own equivalent of taking up the cross. I do not have the right to say that someone else should take a cross.

The resolution of faith is not a logical argument into which everything fits reasonably, but an arduous venture in negation in which conflicting claims, reasonable in their own right, are somehow adjudicated or brought into a livable correlation without achieving full conformity or uniformity of meaning or purpose.

The outcome of the negations -- be it conquest over sin or remorse, the transcendancy of grief, or a total summation of experience against the years of travail and fulfillment -- is never one of total victory and in that sense conclusive. Where the realities of experience are soberly assessed, the mood is always one of assurance tempered with restraint and lingering misgivings. This boundary-line assurance is sufficient, however, to impel one to move toward relinquishment of one's own pressing anxieties and distress, not with a blandishment of naive hope but with trust in God's future.

I reflect, nowadays, on a spirit-mind which broods over the deep for means to penetrate and influence it. We were drawn out of matter because the mind of humanity and of all other intelligent beings is indispensable to that great task of the Holy Spirit which the mind itself can only glimpse and stutter about.

RON:
I began this reflection with some of my decisions for action -- to raise the awareness of seminarians to responsibility in peace and justice, to minister
in the setting of a prison, to be part of a task force
on peace education within an ecumenical consortium, and
to teach a course on peace with justice.

Our reflection forced me to articulate the implicit theology out of which I made these decisions. It
is simply the commandment of love, which I strive to
carry out as a priest within the the context of the Roman Catholic Church which in its institutional structures is both sinful and grace-filled. My decisions have
brought with them the pain of misunderstanding by my
colleagues and the students whom I teach, the experience
of failures, the weariness of over-extension, the
frustrations of academic and institutional regulations.
But as you put it, "resolution and peace are somehow
attain- ed, but not without the price of conflict, pain,
and suffering and not without a sense of taking the
conflict into oneself, of bearing the burden -- in
short, the cross."

> Jack A. Nelson in HUNGER FOR JUSTICE says
> To love God, we must seek justice. To
> love our country, we must seek to over-
> come the corporate, governmental, and
> military policies that victimize the
> bodies and spirits of people at home and
> abroad. What is truly remarkable is that
> human transformation is possible and
> that our lives can make a difference.[5]

I know that I'm an idealist, and I believe that
is all right. My personal faith and my understanding of
the eucharist is what gives me the strength to minister
for peace and to respond to the pleas of the oppressed
and the victims of injustice. The Sacrament of the Eucharist guarantees for me the reality of Jesus' presence
and my union with Him. Each time I celebrate the eucharist and say, "This is my body, this is my blood," it
means to me that I must strive to become like Him --
priest and victim. I must decrease; He must increase.
The Second Vatican Council teaches that the Eucharistic
Sacrifice is the "font and apex of the entire Christian
life." (Lumen Gentium, #11). For me, it is only in the
Eucharist that I find strength to live for peace and
justice.

DAN:

The issue for theological reflection has to do with the reality of evil and the prospects of hope. Peace and justice may even put the Christian into conflict with government policies; you have indicated this in your citation of Jack Nelson. To be Christian sometimes necessitates conflict. Some of our misplaced optimism has been baptized by the cold water of reality. Perhaps Reinhold Niebuhr's realism can help us; certainly, Dietrich Bonhoeffer's courage can give us courage. But theological reflection asks us to believe that we can find our own realistic courage.

More and more, I realize that reflection requires distance. Renewal can only come from people who are not completely tied up with civilization, who are not inwardly crushed by its perplexities. All who have changed the world for better or for worse have had periods of withdrawal from it. Perhaps Lenin and Hitler would never have acquired powers of leadership if they had not been in prison. In the seclusion of Arabia, St. Paul had his soul and mind deepened before becoming the first missionary of Christianity. Our Lord withdrew to the desert for forty days before his active ministry, and often during his life. You withdrew to the solitude of St. Anselm's, a Benedictine Abbey, to put our thoughts together.

We cannot -- most of us -- make that kind of withdrawal. But there is another rhythm of life which we can all follow, distinct from the world's need and yet not indifferent to it. Your personal reflection on Eucharist led me to reflect on the rhythm of the worshipping church, which must become more reflective. It must combine awe with theology and take seriously as Gabriel Fackre puts it, "the dignity of material things and their beneficent interrelationship in opposition to dualistic world views which either disdain subhuman creations or pit human nature against nature."[6]

Joseph Conrad speaks of a "latent feeling of fellowship with all creation."[7] It renews our pleasure in the universe. More than that, our beings touch other beings and let them flow into us. We are mysteriously aware that our own beings have been increased. Something like re-creation runs in us like a tide. The church, through its members -- yes, through you and me -- in worship and Christian action is a tremendous force in that tide that can bring about the peace and justice which is a sign of the Reign of God.

116

Chapter 13
Men and Women in Church Ministry

RON

In our day, the question of men and women in the service of the church becomes the question of women in the church. This is not to say that it is a woman's question, to be addressed and worked through by women alone. No. The issue belongs to everyone in the church, but I emphasize that whereas before our time attention on church leadership has always been upon the priesthood of men in its varying forms, now we turn full attention to the role of women. Contingently, the female role must be known in relationship -- in relationship to men in priesthood and to all persons in the parish.

I am most helped by applying to the strain of my response the paradigm of the Whiteheads; I want to look at the question of ministry in the three ways they suggest for all theological reflection: experience, tradition, and culture. When we have some convergence within the data from all these sources, we have a direction which is a theological response.

Let me begin by following up my own experience. An only child -- an only son -- my experience of responsibility begins with the requirement that I be concerned, alone, with the wellbeing of my parents as they grew older. That care and willing duty continues. I was educated by priests and then I, myself, took on the priesthood and a teaching ministry. I am emotionally and intellectually committed to the life of the priesthood as understood by the Roman Catholic Church. Subject to the magisterial authority of the church, I take this priesthood to mean a celibate life reserved for men who alone may carry the ecclesiastical responsibility for Christ.

In my ministry, I have supervised women and I have worked with women as my associates in the teaching ministry. Each of these persons has enlarged my perception of the possibilities of partnership, and uniquely each described special capabilities which complemented the work I could do.

I have known capable persons who exercised lead-

117

ership and challenged me. They, perhaps especially through their own shared pain, have helped me to know better the experiences of our parishioners. Not afraid to make their understandings known, they have worked for change and for the recognition of "the other voice" in ministry. Often they felt oppressed and I have tried to understand this. Frequently, they have been angry out of frustration, perhaps, but I have come to realize that this anger is probably more than frustration -- that it lies near to despair because of their assessment of intransigence in the institutional church. With these women I have been faced with issues of justice as they never came so close to me before, and I have seen the products of raw anger as it leads to division and soreness in the body of believers.

At the same time, my meeting now with the less aggressive woman parishioner is more sensitive as I try to see how she is affected by the ferment around her. She and I have in common our effort to understand the activity towards equality carried out by convinced women who know, for themselves, that their ministries are valid. Yet the "typical" parishioner, herself a woman, is touched by the insights currently telling her that she, too, has a kind of worth she had not before understood. Though she may have believed herself fulfilled in her specialized and set-aside role, she now gets glimmers that all of the role-making of our generation can and should be open to her. This is an excitement and it is a threat. She treads slowly and steps back periodically to be sure that she wants all that is coming along to her.

In these experiences of mine I, too, have conflicting responses; some are of love and admiration for the vitality and authenticity I see, but some are, frankly, of jealousy and anger for the upsetting of "my" world and the proposed sharing of "my" vocation. Furthermore, I am being invited to reframe all I have understood to be my own priestly commitment. And the church I have loved......what is it now?.....where is it now? As a man ordained a priest, I do not have the freedom to ignore issues as they come or to ignore as inconsequential the concerns of half the population who are equal members in the body of Christ.
This is my experience

The Whiteheads' second point of exploration is culture. In my case the culture is both church and world. My church's world has given me a male society. I was schooled in it, I live in it, I serve in it. I intend to serve everyone, but I do not function within an open culture. Such high celebrations that we witness in certain cycles of the church as the elevation of our Archbishop to Cardinal (recently, 1985, celebrated in Boston) remind us how male our church culture is. The ceremony, the adornment, and the sacrament are entirely for men -- men who are in that moment described as different, entirely, from the rest of humanity because they are the descendents of Peter, the true emissaries of God, and the right emblems for Jesus Christ.

This description serves as the setting of my tradition, as well, but it is important to underline how cultural the Roman Catholic experience is. There is a milieu of "isness" about the ceremonial and sacramental role of priest which belongs to the way life is lived as Catholics -- inside and outside the church or cathedral. Bound as it has been to ethnicity, that cultural quality includes the pervasiveness of ritual "on the block" or in the neighborhood wherever Catholics live, and it has been colored by the ethnic festivals which further tied together persons of Catholic faith. In all of it is the figure of the priest, the one fully committed to this cultural and sacramental world -- yet the one uncommitted to the particulars of worldly relationship -- who is there for the people and for Christ.
This aspect is cultural.

Yet the Whiteheads' third point, tradition, is very close to what I have said about culture. Tradition, for the Catholic, interjects itself into the culture, and tradition, itself, takes on the hues of culture. In our attempt to isolate tradition as the Whiteheads have done, we find the theological underpinnings of culture. We find the belief structure that has an incredible history of its own, adding accretions along the years, yet always attempting to be faithful to the earliest ways of worship and learning. Tradition takes us to the great Fathers of early thought, to the enormous places of worship throughout the world, to the tomes of interpretation, to the communities of men and women who have yearned more than anything to emulate the Christian character as they saw it in Jesus. Continuity is the aspect of this tradition, and diversity is its experience; color and ritual are its form, and sombre stylelessness is its depth. For many, this tradition with the cultures into which it has been grafted, is everything. It is for me.

But I have left out something. All of this "story" alludes to a very closed system in which Catholicity is endemic. Yes, it has been for me. But there is more. My culture, for instance, is also the neighborhoods comprising my city, the news on the television, the cross-cultural and cross-ecclesiastical experiences that are mine daily. These all speak to me of an integrated world in which women have contemplated equally as deeply as men and have discovered their rightness for all of life's work and pleasure.

And my experience bears out what this part of my culture has been saying. I know to be true what women write and say. They say these things about truth to me and they act out their capabilities and dedication in my presence. I only begin to understand that this kind of truth of equality when not fully experienced in a whole segment of society is known as oppression, or repression. It is psychologically and politically incomplete; it is spiritually uneven, truly despairing. Women testify to the fact that their struggles in this culture have had profound effects upon their spirituality; their experience of the Creator MUST be somehow mirrored in the created.

So my theological reflection has brought me to feel deeply for others whose life patterns are so much different from mine, but not much different in their yearnings or their quest for the Eternal One. How do I integrate this as I remain in the priesthood? I, myself, am changed by my understanding, but I am not changed in my being. I am a priest.

It seems to me that in our cultural context, we can do at least two things. We can (1.)develop new interpretations of our symbols and (2.)we can make clearer our use of terminology. To begin, let me take up the second point.

We are in the habit in intermixing the words leadership and priesthood and the words equality, justice, and power. Much of the struggle and soreness in the church is over shared power and leadership. How can this be made fair?

Equality is a human right; that all creation is always regarded by God as whole and lovable gives to each of us humans the right to be considered equal to everyone else. It is a matter of justice that no one is passed over. This is different, though, from the opportunities we are given to express our equality before

120

God. Within the culture and tradition of the Catholic Church, such particular embodiments of our natures and our individual talents are not justice issues but leadership issues. We can be equal before God while following different paths of authority. This is the arena in which I consider the issue of ordination for women.

Stated another way, justice does not demand ordination, a specific expression of power and authority. No, justice demands equal chances for the use of leadership, for the entrance into power structures. Each of those leadership positions is not always fully powerful; again in Catholic culture, ordination does not always mean leadership nor does leadership require ordination. This I think the church is beginning to see. I am. Chaplaincy, pastoral ministers, tribunal officials, chancery workers are roles giving to women equal opportunity to educate and form pastors.

The heart of the matter, though, is theological. Our imagery and our theological reflection is in a male mode. I, a priest, have to take some responsibility for that because it is in my predecessors that this model began and it is in my present that it can be reinterpreted. New interpretations have begun and, indeed, have happened in part throughout our history. Think of Juliana of Norwich. In the fourteenth century she could say "And thus I saw that God rejoiceth that he is our Father, and God rejoiceth that he is our Mother......"[1] This typology of God as both mother and father has become easier for us to use as Pope John Paul I in a 1978 Sunday talk expressed God in this way.

I am, though, more interested in the further explication of the Trinity. Although at least one Holy Father has expressed human relationship to God as like knowing mother and father, the doctrine of the Trinity has been known in male terms. God is Father, is known through Son, and is experienced as Spirit. But some theologians are beginning to focus on the feminine within the Godhead by looking to the Holy Spirit. "Woman symbolizes the response of love to God -- a response which in the depth of godhead is the Holy Spirit."

Yves Congar is helpful to me.[2] He says that

the Spirit's maternity in regard to the Head of the church continues to be exercised in regard to its members: **Pentecost was for the Church what the Annun-**

121

ciation was for Christ (boldface type mine).

I hear Congar's warning, too, that while it is important to give to women equal roles -- allowing the church to become more fully feminine and masculine -- the church must be wary of locking away these roles so that women are defined as charming and passive; the danger was personified in a priest's words to a woman, "You are present as the poetic and loving dimension of the church." Not entirely.

If in the Roman Catholic tradition man is to image God as Christ, the Second Person of the Trinity, then it makes sense that woman is to image God as the Holy Spirit, the Third Person of the Trinity. As Jesus is priest, so man as priest is configured to Christ by sacramental ordination and serves as a sacrament of Christ. As the Holy Spirit is source of life, unity, joy, and motherly love, so woman as consecrated religious serves as the sacrament of the Holy Spirit.

There is mystery in the way the Trinity happens in our lives. My belief that humankind was created in the image of the Triune God leads me to the conclusion that both man as man and woman as woman are theophanous and share in the equality which they image. I am, in the end, left with this mystery and content to leave it there. It gives me the insight to understand the Roman Docaumen "Inter Insigniores" (published January 28, 1977) which states:

> The Church, in its fidelity to the example of its Lord, does not consider itself authorized to admit women to sacramental ordination.

If women were to be ordained priests, the sacramental expression of their very nature would be lost. Women sacramentalize the Holy Spirit and not Christ.

The end of my reflection, though, is in action. Where I am -- in the teaching ministry -- I shall work on the conscientization of my students so that they may give concern, both in their theology and in their working relationships, to their own roles in creating equality of leadership. I, myself, write these words as resolutions for my own modeling in collaborative possibilities, neither my students nor I forgetting the portion of pain that we, by our very being as priests, take into our ministries. To recognize myself as priest-healer and priest-carrier-of-the-mysteries that are God-given through Christ (as well as priest-dominant and priest-unlike-the-mysteries carried by the Holy Spirit) is a moment of truthfulness. I am still in the shadow of its meaning.

DAN
I consider the issue of women's ministry to be a central concern for the church -- an issue, not a question. By that I mean that it is an unresolved matter about which we are compelled to be concerned, but there is no question about its importance or, for me, its outcome. That my denomination has ordained women for at least one hundred years is not a cause for satisfaction so much as the realization of a scar because our history of acceptance is belied by the statistics that demonstrate our reluctance to take this history seriously. We have allowed tradition, culture, and some theologies to weigh down the imperative.

My culture likewise says two things to me. John Stuart Mill in his essay, "The Subjection of Women," argued with vigor and imagination one hundred years ago for the extension of the franchise to women and the ending of legal subordination of married women to their husbands. In England and in this country, however, those things did not happen until women, themselves, took to the podium and the streets in behalf of their own cause.

What have we done better in the church? The same arguments of stridency, inappropriate behavior, waiting for the "right" time, the division of labor are brought into the discussion over women in the pulpit as they were over women in the ballot box. Did we learn nothing? Are we Christians, in fact, no more than very delayed mirrors of our culture?

Tokenism has allowed me to say that I stand in a tradition that takes women's leadership seriously. It has, until lately, been only tokenism. We have heard from the tradition and culture, but we have not in the Whiteheads' model put with them theological reflection.

I read Genesis 1 and 2 as a doctrine of equal creation, as a tale of the high fulfilling on earth of God's activity. This is a first incarnation, and in the travail of men and women throughout Hebrew times, we

123

come ready to receive God's own person with yet an explicit message for our lives. Even in the pre-Christian, all the signs of equality were evident; hints of the timbre of eternal love are found throughout the imagery of the everlasting arms, the love between woman and man, the care of mother for child, the regard of father for son, the early steps of childhood, the symbolism of youth and age. In some places, as in the wisdom literature -- especially Proverbs 8 -- wisdom is clearly female.

These ancient attempts to describe, even in a patriarchal society, a wiser God have led us now to ask whether we have come to a time when we do not have to anthropomorphize God at all. Most of us like to say we have gone beyond finding God "in the garden" or "in heaven," but when we need to ascribe to God the maleness or femaleness -- or both -- of our own creation, have we not just extended or sophisticated the same issue? Will we soon be ready to say that our poor facility for illumination will always require us to **describe** God in our image, while we acknowledge that we are then not defining God? We are children putting words to the unspeakable, not having learned how strong is our temptation to worship our words instead of the mystery behind them.

Krister Stendahl in his work, THE BIBLE AND THE ROLE OF WOMEN IN THE CHURCH,[3] has seen Galatians 3:28 as a breakthrough in the early church. In the words

> Baptized into union with him, you have
> all put on Christ as a garment. There is
> no such thing as Jew and Greek, slave
> and freeman, male and female; for you
> are all one person in Christ Jesus

Stendahl finds a theological statement which is a mandate for the future of the church.

For those of us who began ministry decades ago, a wrench out of our former ways is imperative. The tugging at our comfortable habits cannot be minimized; neither can it be avoided. Why do we look on such a wrench from former behaviors as an attack on ourselves? Isn't it really an opening to new configurations of leadership?

Clearly, the sifting-out period will uproot many of us from behaviors we have assumed, but it does not need to diminish us. It is only a worldly kind of balan-

cing that says human relationships function on a weigh-
scale so that adding to one diminishes another. Giving
in to a new idea does not make me smaller. No. In God's
economy, just as love given to more than one does not
diminish love given to THE one, equality spread over all
human creatures does not have to diminish opportunity
for each (unless we allow it).

We learn from perceptive women leaders and writers. We men ought to be grateful for their guiding and
find in their work the outgrowth of our biblical faith.
The universality of the gospel itself undermines all
justification for the dominance of any group. The
apostle Paul makes plain that baptism frees us from all
false divisions for appreciation of our true unity (a-
gain, the Galatians text). I am drawn to the practical
aspects of this testimony. The Education and Ministry
unit of the National Council of Churches provides us
with an inclusive language lectionary, and everywhere
hymns are sensitively "bent" to render more carefully
the breadth of our imagery.

Improved female/male understanding is not just a
leadership question that is seen through ordination
practice. It comes before every congregation most evi-
dently in the weekly service of thanks and praise. My
experience as a pastor confirms this reality. I have to
take responsibility for building the service with care,
and I have to learn other ways to be wary of my language
in and out of the pulpit. Personification of roles is
actually done at the local level. What women think of
themselves is set locally, and the way in which men regard women's leadership is tempered there. It is not
enough to say that most of those women and men whom we
love in our parishes do not carry placards or even care
especially for the new emphases. We all know parishioners who tell us they are comfortable with the "old" language and roles. We pay them tribute for their dedication and hard work; they are often the saints of the
church.

But we all learn. And leadership is called to
just that task. In my tradition, I am called as pastor
and teacher, as leader. In that calling, I am not expected to look only at the past but at the future, so if
my parishioners do not notice what I see, I am called to
be a skillful leader into the future. I am required by
conscience to notice and set forth, to study and proclaim, to be inclusive in word and deed.

125

The essence of that proclamation on the subject of leadership in the church is, for me, yet becoming. It is clear, however, that styles of leadership are on the threshold of discovery. I am led to Letty Russell, particularly, and her suggestion that partnership is the right configuration. In partnership, she does not mean equality of role or sameness of responsibility; she is searching within the partnered responsibility for a give and take of chores, for an analysis of strengths, for a reassessment of the possibilities in the present. Emphatically, this means that no calling is closed to anyone on the basis of gender. Partnership is not static. It takes seriously the growth of each and the presence in each of the mind of Christ. Who can say what God will still unfold?

There may be something, too, in the idea of androgyny. Our co-writer, Jean, in a lecture at our theological school, has observed the following:

> Clearly, theological thought has come to lean toward the idea of partnership as a concept rich with possibilities but not yet fully arrived. I wonder if androgyny is not the way for us to explore. In androgyny there is a kind of partnership inside the self. All of us who are inveterate test-takers -- whether the formal kind under school or clinical auspices or more popular ones in magazines -- acknowledge ourselves to be a peculiar blend of those characteristics often primarily considered male and those often considered primarily female. Androgyny does not describe us as devoid of gender characteristics but as richly diverse with possibilities derived from our own quite particular combination of personality and ability.

> Androgyny is frightening to many persons who see it as a weakening of their particularity, a flattening-out of the differences that make all of us interesting. (We have the STAR TREK image of the slim jumpsuited and helmeted talking heads.) Androgyny, though, does not change or take away sexuality; it finely describes the attributes of sexuality by returning to us our created capacity of

being unique -- entirely different from **anyone** else, even anyone of our own gender.

"The principle which regulates the existing relations between the two sexes is wrong in itself and is now the chief hindrance to human improvement; and it ought to be replaced by a principle of perfect equality, admitting no power or privilege on the one side, nor disability on the other."[4]

It is an interesting phenomenon that as we humans become better acquainted with a person or place, we pass through phases of understanding that are not on a straight line upward to appreciation.

The Novotnys have spent more than a decade in an English summer course; our initial open-mouthed wonder expressed our experience with the miniature size, with the precious loveliness as compared with American grandeur, with the formal classroom scholarship, with the frank friendliness apparent under the clipped accent. Communication was easy because of the shared language, so it was several years before we realized that there are significant differences between our countries -- that, indeed, we were in a foreign land. Even the language which at first seemed simply pronounced differently became an adventure into new meanings and usage. But the phenomena that separated us, and showed ever more clearly as the years went by, were invitations instead of barriers, endearments instead of rebuffs, charming instead of disenchanting. Now the friendship is full and grateful; it has been fed by our distinctions.

Everyone who has been in a longtime personal relationship can testify to a similar curve in the acquaintance and its fulfillment. Early interest and ardor gives way to steady hope amidst prickly differentiations, and over time the long plain of acceptance and gratitude is approached with fondness.

Our ecumentical friendship has followed a like curve. We have held a fascination for each other's tradition and an academic/religious expectation that they could be placed together fruitfully. Nearly a decade of periodic teaching assignments have revealed both wells of sustenance and deep clefts of diversity. Through all, we have mutual cordiality, regard, and affection.

You readers will have seen the evidence of this "ecumenical curve." Through the text are our variety of language and organization; we have attempted to amalgamate this. In places we are frank to say we cannot speak with one voice even in separate vocabularies, but we have believed it is fair to go ahead with our presentation and lay before you the diverging approaches. We close on a note of unity which, we hope, is actually the mood of the whole book. We are one in Christ, and we have known that faith in our work and in our worship, in our classroom and in our separate places of praise, in our friendship and in our sacramental calling.

. . . .

In the faith we sing together, Christians have come close to one another. Ironically and sadly, the faith we articulate in words has drawn a line between us on many historical occasions. But adoration, hope, praise, longing, conviction, and zeal given in shared verse and choral line have touched the veil of oneness. In song, ecumenical transcendent faith has gone beyond our parochialisms.

Trinitarians sing the Unitarians' "In the Cross of Christ I Glory." Protestants sing the hymn of the Catholic Faber: "There's a Wideness in God's Mercy like the Wideness of the Sea." All, Protestant and Catholic, sing Luther's "A Mighty Fortress is Our God." Orthodox Christians sing the Quaker's "Dear Lord and Father of Mankind."

Everyone joins in hymns written by poets whose names are unknown, persons who perhaps belonged to no church at all. These include "Come Thou Almighty King," "Adeste Fidelis," "Fairest Lord Jesus," "Jesus, the Very Thought of Thee," and "The Strife is O'er, the Victory Won."

Underneath this fact of our shared hymnody is a disposition of anonymity. Lyrics to the musical works we share are not attributed, even when known, as are composers' names or poets of spoken verse. Oh, they are there at the head of the hymn page, but when we refer to a hymn in conversation, we usually call it by its tune name or by the first line; only those who make a study of hymns remember who wrote that line. It is as though the sung stanza is just thrown into the universe.

One could say that this happens after writings are known long enough to have entered the public domain, to have become "classical" pieces, to have lost their author's personality. But we think it applies in somewhat the same way to contemporary writers. They are modern, yes, and they need, for livelihood, to insist on their legal rights of due recompense, and frequently

they are known for a certain thrust in their themes. Yet
they, too, are prodigal. They give us broad and
luxurient imagery which, set to a musical theme, lift
our hearts, minds, and will without reference to their
human presence. Isn't that quintessential religious
motive?

In our impersonal world wherein many are striving in various ways for ego satisfaction -- insisting
on their ways, wanting children to emulate their style
of living, wanting to be heard at every meeting, wanting
to publish every year -- we desperately need gifted persons who are secure enough with vocation, children, and
the universe so they are willing to be, so to speak,
anonymous. It takes a kind of mystical sense to do this.

We think of the hymn, "Our God to Whom We Turn."
The music is J.S. Bach's - strong with melancholy overtones. But the words.....

> Our God, to whom we turn
> When weary with illusion,
> Whose stars serenely burn
> Above this earth's confusion,
> Thine is the mighty plan,
> The steadfast order sure
> In which the world began,
> Endures, and shall endure.[1]

Some hymns can work with many tunes, but this one seems
wed to the demanding relentlessness of the one named
STEADFAST. How modern is the weariness with clever manipulative illusions; how clear that our souls have no
rest until, as in the words of the second verse, "truth
from falsehood part."

In a performance by the New York Philarmonic
Orchestra under the direction of Leonard Bernstein, the
musicians who were following that Jewish conductor were
people with backgrounds in Eastern Orthodox Russia, in
Lutheran Germany, in Roman Catholic Italy, in mideast
Jewry and Islam, and in Protestant America. Their differences melted away under the impact of a common love
for music and a consuming desire to give out as faith-
fully as possible the majestic compositions entrusted to
them.

Consider the Second Symphony of Charles Ives in
thinking about the integrative force of music. That New
England Congregationalist and outstanding businessman in

the insurance world gave us a musical autobiography which combined themes of music he had heard as a boy in "typical" New England communities. We catch traces of Saturday night's dance music, of July Fourth's hometown celebrations with "Columbia, the Gem of the Ocean," of boyhood church sounds like "When I Survey the Wondrous Cross," and of family music hours around the piano with the strains of Stephen Foster.

It is likely that our faith is a symphony, in which my single note may only be the tingle of the triangle. We need the meditative flutes, the singing violins, the clean-sounding trumpet, and the rumbling bass viol -- and the sporadic piccolo peep or triangle ting. I may have to wait for the right moment when my part is called by our transcendent conductor.

Harry Emerson Fosdick preached that vital religion is like good music. It needs no defense, only rendition. A wrangling controversy in support of religion is as if the members of the orchestra should beat the folks over the head with their instruments to prove that music is beautiful.

Music helps to bring reconciliation to the varying emphases in faith. There are modes of faith that require harmony and the reconciliation of an emerging dominant theme. Theology alone has difficulty in doing this. Certainly, it would be hard to claim that diligent theological work provides a strong guarantee that the church will manage to go beyond religious semantic battles into faith. The reverse is often the case: theology easily becomes ideological. At times, it provides arguments by which churches can display malice, pettiness, and all uncharitableness towards their neighbors -- and do so with good conscience. We can, too, believe that theology is an end in itself, leading us to thinking that a satisfactory theological formulation is substitutionary, not preliminary, to action in hope.

The sung faith makes it possible for people to receive the ministrations of the church in almost anonymous fashion and then to move out strengthened by them into the wider life of the world, nourished as by the rendition of a great symphony.[2]

. . . .

It is a powerful experience to stand by a stream, miles away from the sea coast, and catch the

132

scents of the infinite ocean. It is a greater experience to stand by the stream of human life as it flows and catch in it again and again the "murmurs and scents of the infinite sea" of God, the Eternal One.

The human species is a paradox not because it is inherently both good and evil, but because biologically, socially, and ethically, it has the most adaptable behavior of all living organisms. It is in the movement from contemplation to action and back again that we discover God. Each Christian must pass through the metaphors of faith and the struggles of the world to the mission in unconditional love of God and neighbor.

Introduction

1   Robert McAfee Brown, **Theology in a New Key** (Phila-
    delphia: The Westminster Press, 1978), p. 11.
2   Andrew Martin Fairbairn, **The Philosophy of the
    Christian Religion** (New York: The MacMillan Co.,
    1902), pp. 299-300.
3   Edward Schillebeeckx, **Ministry: Leadership in the
    Community of Jesus Christ** (New York: Herder and Her-
    Herder, 1981), p. 3.
4   Karl Rahner, **Theology of Pastoral Action** (New York:
    Herder and Herder, 1968), p. 29

First Part   THE STUDIO IN WHICH WE WORK
      SECTION I   Artistic Materials We are Given
          Chapter 1   Process and Language

1   Schubert M. Ogden, "What is Theology?" **The Journal
    of Religion**, I:1 (Chicago: University of Chicago
    Press, 1972), p. 22.
2   Ibid., pp. 32-33.
3   Lawrence Thompson, **Robert Frost, The Years of Tri-
    umph 1915-1928** (New York: Holt, Reinhart, Winston,
    1970), p. 65.

          Chapter 2   Matter for Theological Reflection

1   See Seward Hiltner, preface to **Pastoral Theology**
    (New York: Abingdon Press, 1958).
2   Ibid., p. 222, note 19.
3   Frank W. Cushwa, **An Introduction to Conrad** (New
    York: The Odyssey Press, 1933), p. 225.
4   Milton Mayeroff, **On Caring** (New York: Harper and Row
    Publishers, 1971, Perennial Library, 1972), p. 1.
5   Ibid., p. 30.
6   For a vivid example of one person's self-examination
    around the concepts of self-seeking and self-sacri-
    fice, consult Dag Hammerskjold, **Markings**, trans.
    Leaf Sjoberg and W. E. Auden (New York: Alfred A.
    Knopf, 1964).
7   Mayeroff, **Caring**, pp. 54-69.
8   Karl Rahner and Herbert Vergrimler, eds., **Theologi-
    cal Dictionary** (New York: Seabury Press, 1973),
    pp. 320-321.

9   Karl Rahner, **Theological Investigations**, no. 6, trans. Karl Kruger and Boniface Kruger (New York: The Seabury Press, 1974), pp. 231-252.
10 Langdon Gilkey, **How the Church can Minister to the World without Losing Itself** (New York: Harper and Row, 1964).
11 Dorothee Soelle, **Beyond Mere Obedience** (New York: Pilgrim Press, 1982).
12 Viktor E. Frankl, **The Will to Meaning** (New York: The New American Library Inc., 1969), p. 16.
13 Rahner and Vergrimler, **Dictionary**, p. 354.

Chapter 3   Occasions for Theological Reflection

1   See Anton T. Boisen, **The Exploration of the Inner World: A Study of Mental Disorders and Religious Experience** (New York: Willett, Clark and Co., 1936).
2   The Reverend Ronald J. Gariboldi's reflection on the occasion of the death of his father in 1979.
3   Rollo May, **My Quest for Beauty** (Dallas: Saybrook Press, 1985), p. 141.
4   Reinhold Niebuhr, "Humour and Faith," **Discerning the Signs of the Times** (New York: Charles Scribner's Sons, 1946), pp. 111-131.
5   See table of contents in Letty M. Russell, **The Future of Partnership** (Philadelphia: The Westminster Press, 1979).
6   Dietrich Bonhoeffer, **Letters and Papers from Prison** (New York: Macmillan and Co., 1967), pp. 281, 286, 300.

Chapter 4   An Instance: Doctrine of Revelation

1   See C. S. Lewis, **That Hideous Strength** (London : Pan Books, 1955).
2   Rahner, "Experience of Transcendence," **Investigations**, no. 18, trans. Edward Quinn (New York: Crossroad, 1983), pp. 132-142.
3   For a consideration of John Henry Newman's concept of development, see Jan Hendrik Walgrave, **Unfolding Revelation** (Philadelphia: Westminster Press, 1972), pp. 293-313.
4   See Karl Barth, **Natural Theology** (London: Baillie and Martin, 1946).
5   Avery Dulles, **Models of Revelation** (Garden City: Doubleday, 1983), pp. 27-28.

6   Thomas Merton, **No Man is an Island** (New York: Doubleday Image Books, 1967), p. 120.
7   Robert Moffatt, **The Thrill of Tradition** (London: SCM Press, 1944), p. 112.
8   Ibid.
9   Dulles, **Models**, pp. 116-117.

    SECTION II   Sources of Light for Our Work
        Introduction

1   James D. Whitehead and Evelyn Eaton Whitehead, **Method in Ministry** (New York: The Seabury Press, 1980).

        Chapter 5   Anthropology

1   See Rahner, "Brief Theological Observations on the State of Fallen Nature," **Investigations**, vol 19, pp. 39-53.
2   John W. Dixon, Jr., **The Physiology of Faith** (New York: Harper and Row, 1979), p. 30.
3   Poem by John Masefield, Poet Laureate of England.
4   Michael Casey, "St. Benedict's Approach to Prayer," **Cistercian Studies** 15 (1980): 328.
5. Adrian van Kaam, **In Search of Spiritual Identity** (Denville, New Jersey: Dimension Books, 1984).
6   Primarily described in Paul Tillich, **Systematic Theology** vol. 1 (Chicago: University of Chicago Press, 1957), p. 53.
7   Reinhold Niebuhr, **Moral Man and Immoral Society** (New York: Charles Scribner's Sons, 1932).

        Chapter 6   Culture

1   Barbara Watts Hargrove, "Modernity and Its Disadvantages: The Cultural Context of Theological Education," **Theological Education,** vol. 20, no. 1 (1983).
2   Samuel Hoffenstein, **The Complete Poetry of Samuel Hoffenstein** (New York: Modern Library, 1954),p. 212.
3   E. H. Robertson, **Paul Schneider, The Pastor of Buchenwald** (Chicago: S.C.M. Book Club, 1956), p. 7.
4   see Dietrich Bonhoeffer's **Letters**.
5   Josef Peiper, **Leisure, the Basis of Culture** (New York: New American Library, 1952), p. 17.

Chapter 7   Ecclesiology

1   Rahner, "Basic Communities," **Investigation,** pp. 159-165. Rahner describes Action 365, a group of ecumenically constituted Christian basic communities who intend commitment to the third world through service.
2   Robert Frost, "Revelation," **The Pocket Book** of **Robert Frost's Poems** (New York: The Washington Square Press, 1946), p. 155.

SECTION III   Media
Chapter 8   The Bible and Theological Reflection

1   Jan Hendrik Walgrave, **Unfolding Revelation** (Philadelphia: Westminster Press, 1972), p. 392.
2   Jacques Gagne, "A Model of Theological Reflection for Seminarians." An unpublished paper presented for a class at Andover Newton Theological School, Newton Centre, MA, 1980.
3   A. B. Bruce, **The Parabolic Teaching of Christ** (New York: A. C. Armstrong Sons), p. 120.
4   In Eugene Wehrli, **Explaining the Parables** (Philadelphia: The United Church Press, 1963).
5   Robert E. Neale, **Loneliness, Solitude, and Companionship** (Philadelphia: Westminster Press, 1984), p. 128.
6   Rahner, "Experience of the Holy Spirit," **Investigations,** vol. 18, p. 207.

Chapter 9   Sacrament and Theological Reflection

1.   For a detailed study of the concept of "sacrament," see Ronald J. Gariboldi, **Caring Relationships with the Institutionalized Elderly** (Ann Arbor: University MicroFilms, 1976).
2   Huston Smith made this observation in a lecture at The University of New Hampshire, sometime in the early 60's.

Second Part   THE CONTEXT
SECTION I   People - the Artists
Chapter 10   General Theories

1   Maria Harris, **Teaching and Religious Imagination** (New York: Harper and Row, 1986).

2   Martin Buber, **Between Man and** Man (New York: Macmillan Books, 1965), p. 100.
3   William Temple, entry for September First, **Daily Readings from William Temple,** compiled Hugh Warner, (London: Hodder and Stoughton, 1948), p. 128.

Chapter 11   Some Theorists

1   Bernard Lonergan, **Method in Theology** (New York: The Seabury Press, 1979).
     For an excellent analysis of Lonergan's method in relation to our discipline of theological reflection, see the Doctor of Ministry thesis for Catholic University by Christine Partisano, **Development and Implementation of a Reflection Process for Ministerial Education/Formation** based on Lonergan's "Method" and Erickson's "Life Cycle" (Ann Arbor: University Microfilms International, 1983).
2   Whitehead and Whitehead, **Method.**
3   Robert Kinast, "A Process Model of Theological Re-Reflection," **Journal of Pastoral Care** (June, 1983).
4   Peter Henriot, S.J. and Joe Holland, **Social Analysis: Linking Faith and Justice** (Washington: Center of Concern, 1980).
5   James Fowler, **Stages of Faith** (San Francisco: Harper and Row, 1981), p. xii.
6   Douglas Steere, **On Being Present Where You Are,** a Pendle Hill Pamphlet (Lebanon, Pennsylvania: Sowers Printing Company, 1967).
7   Letty M. Russell, **The Future of Partnership** (Philadelphia: Westminster Press, 1979).
8   Dorothee Soelle, **The Strength of the Weak** (Philadelphia: Westminster, 1984), p. 81.
9   See Edward Robinson, **The Original Vision** (New York: Seabury Press, 1983). The book reports on the religious experience of childhood, the fruit of work done at the Religious Experience Research Unit at Manchester College in Oxford. As John Westerhoff says in the introduction to this American edition (p. ix), "few existing books offer greater insights for understanding religious life and spiritual awareness or suggest greater consequences for shaping a theory of religious education."
10   Ibid., p. 19.

SECTION II   The Settings for Reflection
      Chapter 12   Places: Academy, Parish, Journal

1   W. Shelton, **Psychology and the Promethean Will** (New
    York: Harper & Brothers, 1936), quoted by Huston
    Smith in R. Prichard, editor, **Principles of Quality
    Teaching at University Level** (Columbia, South Caro-
    lina: University of South Carolina Press, 1974).
2   This case study is taken from the class notes of
    Ronald J. Gariboldi in a course given at St. Meinrad
    School of Theology, Indiana, in June, 1983.

        Chapter 13   Habits: Tutorial, Biography,
                              Supervision

1   George Bailey, "At the University," in **C. S. Lewis:
    Speaker and Teacher** (London: Hodder & Stoughton,
    1971).
2   Martin Buber, **Man and Man**, p. 95.
    See also I **and Thou**, trans. Walter Kaufman (New
    York: Scribners, 1970)
3   Ibid., p. 101.
4   John Vincze, quoting Aquinas, in a class presenta-
    tion at Andover Newton.
5   Helmut Thielicke, **A Little Exercise for Young Theol-
    ogians** (Grand Rapids: Eerdman's Publishing Co),
    Co.), 1962)
6   This was the experience of Daniel Novotny during a
    pastorate in Belmont, Massachusetts.
7   Bonhoeffer, **Letters.**
8   Martin Luther King, Jr., **Stride Toward Freedom** – **The
    Montgomery Story** (San Francisco: Harper and Row,
    1958).
9   Ibid., p. 74.
10 Ibid., p. 80.
11 Martin Luther King, Jr., **Strength to Love** (San Fran-
    cisco: Harper and Row, 1963), p. 126.
12 Ibid.
13 James A. Conlon, **Task Force on Theological Reflec-
    tion and Spiritual Formation** – An Interim Report
    (Toronto: Toronto School of Theology, 1983), p. 1.
14 Lee C. Riggs, "Theological Principles for Supervi-
    sion," an unpublished paper for class at Andover
    Newton, 1978.

SECTION III   Peering in the Window
      Chapter 14   Peace and Justice

1   Archbishop Romero, "Christian Hope: In Death is
     Life," condensed by Sally Scharper from "A Martyr's
     Message of Hope," **Maryknoll Magazine**, March 1984,
     p. 42.
2   Humberto Cardinal Medieros, "Stewards of This Heri-
     tage," **What God Wants** (Boston: St. Paul Editions,
     1984), p. 421.
3   See Reinhold Neibuhr, **The Nature and Destiny of Man**
     (New York: Charles Scribner's Sons, 1953).
4   Gabriel Fackre, **The Religious Right and Christian
     Faith** (Grand Rapids: William B. Eerdman's Publishing
     Co., 1982).
5   Jack A. Nelson, **Hunger for Justice** (Maryknoll, New
     York: Orbis, 1980), p. viii.
6   Fackre, **Religious Right**, p. 42.
7   Cushwa, **Conrad**.

      Chapter 15   Women and Men in Church Ministry

1   Juliana of Norwich, **Revelation of Divine Love** ed.
     Dom Hudlestein, O.S.B. (Westminster: Newman Press,
     1927), p. 103.
2   Yves Congar, "The Spirit as God's Femininity," **The-
     ology Digest** Vo. 30, No. 2, pp. 129-32.
3   Krister Stendahl, **The Bible and the Role of Women in
     the Church** (Philadelphia: Fortress Press, 1966),
     p. 32.
4   John Stuart Mill, "Essay on the Subjection of Wo-
     Women," 1869.

      Conclusion

1   Words by Edward Grubb, 1854-1939.
2   For a fascinating and inspiring treatise on hymns,
     read S. Paul Schilling, **The Faith We Sing** (Phila-
     delphia: Westminster Press, 1983), p. 213.

Ronald Gariboldi is Professor of Pastoral Theology and Director of Field Education at St. John's Seminary in Brighton, Massachusetts.

Daniel and Jean Novotny are members of the Adjunct Faculty and Associates in Field Education at Andover Newton Theological School in Newton Centre, Massachusetts. For twelve years they have directed a summer study session in Oxford, England.

Both schools are members of the Boston Theological Institute, a consortium of nine theological schools in the Boston area.